Neuro-Linguistic Programming for Change Leaders

We know a lot about change leadership. We understand how to design change programmes, and we know how to prescribe best practice change methods. Yet, despite all this knowledge, it is reported that up to 70% of change leadership projects fail to realize many of their objectives. The fault lines are cited as occurring at the *micro* level of social interaction.

What we don't adequately explain and demonstrate within the change leadership literature is *how* change leaders may *consciously generate* in themselves and in others *resourceful* mindsets, emotions, attitudes, and behaviours to enable positive change leadership dynamics. *Neuro-Linguistic Programming for Change Leaders: The Butterfly Effect* fills this gap by connecting the practices of *personal development* with those of *corporate change leadership*.

This book has the vision of advancing NLP as a serious technology in the change leader's tool box. The book introduces to operations managers, HR practitioners, OD specialists, and students of management new ideas and practices, which can transform their effectiveness as change leaders.

It focuses on the benefits of applied NLP to change leaders as a generative change toolkit. Secondly, the book provides a model that shows change leaders how to build a climate of psychological safety to establish rapport with stakeholders. Thirdly, the book provides a strategy for enabling broader cultural change and stakeholder engagement throughout the organization.

Dr David Potter, MBA, PhD, is the founder of The Cultural Change Company, UK, which specializes in enabling successful cultural change interventions to stimulate organizational innovation.

Neuro-Linguistic Programming for Change Leaders
The Butterfly Effect

Dr David Potter, MBA, PhD

LONDON AND NEW YORK

First published 2018
by Routledge
2 Park Square, Milton Park, Abingdon, Oxon OX14 4RN

and by Routledge
711 Third Avenue, New York, NY 10017

Routledge is an imprint of the Taylor & Francis Group, an informa business

© 2018 David Potter

The right of David Potter to be identified as author of this work has been asserted by him in accordance with sections 77 and 78 of the Copyright, Designs and Patents Act 1988.

All rights reserved. No part of this book may be reprinted or reproduced or utilised in any form or by any electronic, mechanical, or other means, now known or hereafter invented, including photocopying and recording, or in any information storage or retrieval system, without permission in writing from the publishers.

Trademark notice: Product or corporate names may be trademarks or registered trademarks, and are used only for identification and explanation without intent to infringe.

British Library Cataloguing-in-Publication Data
A catalogue record for this book is available from the British Library

Library of Congress Cataloging-in-Publication Data
Names: Potter, David, 1963- author.
Title: Neuro-linguistic programming for change leaders : the butterfly effect / David Potter.
Description: Abingdon, Oxon ; New York, NY : Routledge, 2018. | Includes bibliographical references and index.
Identifiers: LCCN 2017057251 (print) | LCCN 2017059058 (ebook) | ISBN 9781315099569 (eBook) | ISBN 9781138297005 (hardback : alk. paper) | ISBN 9781138495999 (pbk : alk. paper)
Subjects: LCSH: Neurolinguistic programming. | Organizational change--Management. | Leadership.
Classification: LCC BF637.N46 (ebook) | LCC BF637.N46 P68 2018 (print) | DDC 158/.9--dc23
LC record available at https://lccn.loc.gov/2017057251

ISBN: 978-1-138-29700-5 (hbk)
ISBN: 978-1-138-49599-9 (pbk)
ISBN: 978-1-315-09956-9 (ebk)

Typeset in Times New Roman
by Taylor & Francis Books

This book is dedicated to my mother Elizabeth, my father Eric, and my sister Denise and all of the teachers and mentors I have had the good fortune to have known. Also to Jens Starke Master NLP Trainer and decent chap from Berlin for believing.

Contents

List of illustrations	ix
Foreword	x
Introduction to the book	xii

PART 1
The theory and operational context of NLP 1

1 Conscious leadership 3

2 NLP as a field of applied sociology 13

3 New management practices: paradigm change 23

4 'The map is not the territory': reframing change leadership 31

5 It starts with oneself: the butterfly effect 40

6 NLP and the Law of Requisite Variety 51

7 The NLP paradigm 64

PART 2
Applied NLP 73

8 Building the case for change 75

9 Building psychological safety 86

10 Un-packing the mindset mix 94

11 Meta-programmes 104

12 Framing of experience 115

13 Caretaking and guiding 126

viii *Contents*

14 A model of rapport building   135

15 Communication models   145

16 NLP and OD: two not-so-distant relatives. It's time for
    collaboration   155

    Index   162

Illustrations

Figures

5.1	Maslow's hierarchy of motivational needs	42
8.1	SOAR Model	78
8.2	Logical Levels	80
8.3	Media statement	81
9.1	Model of rapport building	89
10.1	Wheel of repetitive behaviour	101
11.1	Perceptual Position mapping	112
14.1	A model of rapport processes	139

Tables

4.1	Perceptual filter analysis	32
8.1	SCORE model change diagnostic and action sheet excel services	85
10.1	Mindset mix analysis	96
10.2	Theory X versus theory Y	100
11.1	Meta-programme examples	105
11.2	Meta-programme audit checklist	108
12.1	Stakeholder values and beliefs framework	118
15.1	Meta-model violations: distortions	152

Foreword

A couple of years ago I was asked to deliver a paper on Change Management at a business symposium, and as I was speaking in the afternoon I decided to listen in on earlier speakers, so I could engage with any emerging themes. That decision was such a game changer for me as one of those speakers turned out to be David Potter.

I have been an advocate and practitioner of Neuro-Linguistic Programming (NLP) for over 20 years but, to be honest, I find a great deal of published work to be difficult to apply into everyday work-life. When I heard David speak, he delivered an enthralling presentation which was immediately accessible, practical, and inspirational. From that moment I was keen to learn as much as possible about David's refreshing approach to NLP and its application to support organizational change, leadership development and personal growth. When I heard that David would be writing a book in which he would be sharing his ideas I was delighted!

I genuinely believe that if Human Resource/Organizational Development professionals are to make a meaningful contribution to their business, it is essential that they are considered to be experts on human behaviour, and are equipped with a quiver full of ideas that could support the continued successful development of their business. In this book, David has presented a fantastic distillation of his ability to accessibly communicate his expertise in researching and disseminating novel and meticulously researched themes for the professional practitioner's tool-kit.

There are many fascinating aspects to this book; however, most impressively, David elegantly conveys the key theoretical components of NLP, simultaneously providing practical ideas that can provide any HR/OD practitioner with a guide to achieving more effective organizational change with people placed at the centre of the approach.

David has conveyed a great ability to connect the various theoretical aspects of NLP into accessible, effective everyday language supported by great human insight and observation. David writes with the gravitas and authority of a person in total command of their subject. There is a great need for this book as it offers a comprehensive illustration of how you can bring a new and refreshing approach to organizational and cultural change through the application of NLP. David helps you understand how to use specific techniques to have the maximum impact and encourages you to experiment, be bold, creative, and authentic.

I really do hope that you gain as much from reading this book as I have from David's approach to cultural change. I can think of no better NLP practitioner to learn from with a strong moral and ethical compass – by the end of the book I am sure you will be inspired – I hope you enjoy the adventure and experience!

Leatham

Leatham Green LLM, MBA, ACEL, BA
Public Sector People Management Association HR Director of the Year 2016
HRO Forum HR Global Superstar Award 2018
Founder: The Mindful HR Centre

Introduction to the book

This is a book about change management and the potential for applied Neuro-Linguistic Programming (NLP) to transform the fortunes of change efforts. The book has the vision of breaking down the mystery of NLP and relating its methods and concepts to the practical activity of change management in organizations. A related vision is to advance NLP as a serious technology in the general manager's tool box. The philosophy that will drive the writing is one of introducing to operational managers, HR practitioners, OD specialists and students of management new ideas and practices which can transform their effectiveness as change leaders, educators, and coaches.

The purpose of this book is to provide you with insights into the NLP ideas that can enable the establishment of productive change leadership relationships.

The ability to influence and work cohesively with others are arguably the critical competences that enable successful change leadership. Neuro-Linguistic Programming provides proven methods for enabling the conditions that generate collaboration between change leaders and their teams. The aim throughout this book is to direct you towards a field of practice that has the capacity to unlock the potential for the outstanding leadership potential that you have within you if you know the keys to use.

This book fills a very important gap in what is being taught in business schools throughout the world regarding change leadership. Managers are being taught to think intellectually and abstractly about change leadership. They are being taught how to plan for change. They are taught about the main challenges involved in planning for and leading change. They are being taught how to understand the social and cultural dynamics involved in leading successful change. And, yes, these teachings are important. However, despite this dense catalogue of teaching regarding change leadership there remains general dissatisfaction regarding change leadership results. Something is not working. Something is going against the rational premise that we have studied change management for over 70 years, made the findings readily available and yet change leadership remains a very challenging and problematic aspect of general management.

The issue, it seems, is that managers are not being taught how to understand people, including themselves. They are not being adequately prepared for the searing heat and unpredictable nature of social interaction. They are not

Introduction to the book xiii

being prepared to manage fluctuations in their emotional states. They are expected to live with limiting beliefs and compensate for these with un-resourceful strategies. They struggle with the idea of critical self-reflection. These fault lines impact negatively on the ability of change leaders to lead with influence.

I have practiced management for 25 years. I have led numerous change projects and participated in even more. I have studied up close and personal what happens when managers try to engage with stakeholders during change projects. I have listened to the back-stage conversations of managers and staff making sense of the approach to change leadership on the part of their change managers. I have studied change leadership at Master's and Doctorate level and, yet I also remained dissatisfied regarding what I have learned.

My dissatisfaction lay in the gap between our knowledge of why change leadership efforts often do not work that effectively and how we remedy this situation. I wanted to know how, as a change leader, I could use all the knowledge I had to be a far more effective change leader. I came to realize that what I needed to understand was how to figure people out and this had to start with myself. I had to understand at the micro level of interaction how we make sense of the world around us and decide on our social strategies to act upon the models we create.

I searched for a body of knowledge and practice that specialized in providing practical insights and change interventions into how people tick. I wanted to understand the way that people generate the social results that disrupted change leadership efforts. I also wanted to understand the strategies successful change leaders used. This naturally involved building a bridge between my interest in organizational cultural change and the not un-related field of personal development. One could argue that these two areas of study and practice have been treated as mutually exclusive with the former being scientific and the latter constituting an area of pseudo-science. This presupposition is most unfortunate as they are, in fact, mutually inclusive close intellectual and practical cousins. There is much we can learn about how change leaders can improve their effectiveness by merging a study of both disciplines. The challenge was where to start. I chose to study the area of personal development called 'Neuro-Linguistic Programming' (NLP) and connect this to the literature on leading change in an organization. Why this choice?

We all know that organizational culture is built on concepts such as:

- Beliefs
- Values
- Attitudes
- Behaviours

And we all know that this framework involves two levels of interactions: (1) internal to self, and (2) external to self. These two levels of interactive sense-making are the primary shapers and movers of organizational culture. I knew quite a bit about organizational culture and related change management models.

xiv *Introduction to the book*

What I knew less about was how at the level of the individual change leader I could build a model of 'change' that could smoothly engage and change the broader organizational culture: a model of change practice that works; a model of change practice that has a proven record of accomplishment; and a model that is easily taught to managers and which produces social results very quickly.

The body of knowledge and practice I discovered was NLP. It just felt right to me; the ideas chimed with my experience and when I read the literature I liked the evocative images the prominent authors conjured up in their writings. I was very attracted to this field of knowledge and practice as it seemed to deal with social construction issues, identity work and paradigm construction processes, all of which are the foundations of the cultural change literature. The difference that made the difference was that NLP traded in practical change solutions and focused on the individual and their relationship internal to self and externally to others. This, I felt, had the potential of filling the gap in our knowledge that I think is required.

Because of my curiosity, I have spent the last five years studying and practicing NLP. I have studied with the world's top NLP trainers such as Brian Costello and Steven Burns of the Scottish Centre for NLP and Robert Dilts and Judith Delozier at NLPU based at the University of California Santa Cruz, the spiritual home of NLP. I have worked with over 1,000 managers and students of management teaching NLP across multiple business schools and organizations in the private and the public sectors as well as speaking at conferences on the subject. The conclusion I came to was that as an area of personal development NLP also works with:

- Beliefs
- Values
- Attitudes
- Behaviours
- Identity

NLP provides insights and methods of rapid change and improvement into social processes such as:

- Managing our emotional states.
- Changing limiting beliefs.
- Improving our communication capabilities.
- Changing thinking patterns that were producing poor social results.
- Improving our rapport-building skills and active relationships.
- Improving our influencing skills.
- Dramatically improving our behavioural flexibility.
- Managing stress productively.

I realized that when I built a bridge between the two fields of practice of Organizational Change Management and NLP I could have a significant impact on the capabilities of change leaders to create the organizational culture they really want to belong to. I could enable far more successful change management and leadership outcomes.

The bridge I have built is 'NLP for Change Leaders: The Butterfly Effect', a book on change leadership that can have a serious impact on the future outcomes of change leadership projects. Throughout this book I will share with you dynamic perspectives and skills that will transform your change management and leadership capacities as well as providing you with opportunities for personal growth and transformation. This book is based upon innovative NLP ideas and methods rooted in the creative melting pot of Silicon Valley, California.

The book benefits from the author bringing a solid appreciation of organizational theory wedded to substantial management experience to the body of knowledge and practice of NLP. This mix of expertise is applied to the structure of the book and is highly original in relation to the stock of NLP books currently on the market. I invite you to sit comfortably, go into a relaxed state of mind and enjoy this exploration of NLP and come to appreciate its great potential as an enabler of successful change leadership outcomes. Enjoy this short journey of discovery through the world of NLP and the learnings can and will serve you well. I invite you to be curious and open to the potential for developing your understanding of a highly rewarding area of change management practice that has the potential to transform lives.

This book is a theoretically informed yet highly practical survey of NLP ideas and methods. This book introduces participants to social strategies rooted in NLP that can enable personal change and freedom from limiting beliefs and create 'The Butterfly Effect' in organizations, stimulating systematic change.

It is common knowledge that managing change in organizations is a tough business. We have a rapidly changing staff and customer demographic; millennials are featuring as critical employee resources who expect a particular kind of work experience; traditional leadership models based on authority of position are being rejected. The climate and culture within many organizations are becoming increasingly tense and difficult to manage.

We need different approaches to the ways in which we engage with key stakeholder groups that transcend transactional methods. NLP for change leaders shows managers that they can manage their emotional states, overcome belief barriers, build charisma, leverage leadership skills, and build rapport with stakeholders. It is a beautiful thing. The next section in this introduction will summarize the structure of the book.

Book structure

Part 1: The theory and operational context of NLP

Chapter 1: Conscious leadership

In this chapter I will introduce my definition of the change leader and the specific idea of conscious leadership that will form part of the conceptual and xvi *Introduction to the book*

practical framework to connect with the overarching themes of the book. I will introduce the practical activity of meta-reflection as a core change leadership capability. I have designed a short reflective statement regarding my own change journey as an explanation regarding the motivations behind this book. This chapter is intended to encourage the emergence of the reflective practitioner that lies within all of us involved in leading change initiatives

Chapter 2: NLP as a field of applied sociology

In this chapter I will define NLP based on the definitions which I derived from the work of leading NLP developers and creators. There is no fixed definition of NLP as the field holds many different meanings for many different people. Nevertheless, we need a definition that holds true to the originator's intentions and in this chapter I will offer such a construction. I will briefly, survey the historical roots of NLP to provide you with a sense of accessibility to its development as a field of change practice. Finally, I will consider NLP as a distinctive field of applied sociology with powerful complementary synergies with management science being taught in traditional business schools throughout the world.

Chapter 3: New management practices: paradigm change

An underlying presupposition that guides the writing for this book is that the conscious leadership skills managers require to be effective change leaders are underdeveloped. Conscious leadership skills as catalysts and enablers for the establishment of psychological safety in groups are often ignored as critical training requirements before and during change leadership episodes. This skills deficit leads to fault lines that undermine the potential success of change programmes. This chapter will explore these ideas and review research that helps to identify important issues that conscious change leaders should be aware of. This chapter will also consider the dynamic nature of work and the shift in the cultural profile of both employees and managers. Finally, this chapter will locate NLP as a social change technology with the potential to enable a paradigm shift in management culture towards a model that has a better socio/cultural fit with society at large.

Chapter 4: 'The map is not the territory': reframing change leadership

NLP is ideally suited to enabling conscious change leadership because it is broadly based on social construction processes. The philosophy that underpins conscious change leadership is that '*The map is not the territory*' which basically means all our perceptions are simply maps of a potential reality rather than actual reality – and imperfect maps at best. This is known as an interpretivist ontological position. Ontology is defined as the nature of being (Tsoukas & Chia, 2002). The contrast to interpretivist is positivist which assumes that reality is accessible in an objective sense and can be measured, and underlying principles identified for analysis (Denzin, 2001). As conscious change leadership involves how one manages one's subjective experience and that of others an interpretivist approach offers greater flexibility. This is because organizational change works through social construction processes which can be managed more effectively if we have ways of working with our internal representations of reality constructed within the theatre of our minds. This chapter will consider conscious change leadership as a process of reconstructing our mental models of the world as we perceive it. NLP as a change technology is ideally suited to support such a project which is called reframing. Throughout this chapter I will review two models of change leadership: (1) The transmission model; and, (2) the diffusion model, and compare these with the goal of inviting change leaders to reframe their unconscious model of change leadership and relate this process to NLP techniques. The concept of *'everyday reframing'* as a significant conscious change leadership process will be examined and connected with NLP applications.

Chapter 5: It starts with oneself: the butterfly effect

In this chapter I will consider the deeply personal nature of NLP and argue that all changes in behaviours or values and beliefs within an organization start with the self. Organizations are socio-cultural systems and are characterized by the butterfly effect which dictates that a change in one part of the system will result in a vibration throughout the culture that creates systematic change. NLP is a valuable personal development toolkit as well as a resource to enable broader behavioural change. This chapter will also consider unconscious and conscious modelling as a transmission strategy for inculcating preferred leadership styles throughout an organization. I will take our preferred leadership style, conscious change leadership, as the working model and explain how this can be taught at both conscious and unconscious levels of learning to others throughout the organization.

Chapter 6: NLP and the Law of Requisite Variety

This chapter will review the operating philosophy that NLP is built around which could be categorized under the meta-idea *'The Law of Requisite Variety'*. NLP has a conceptual structure around which its capacity for practice as a change methodology is enabled. I call this the *'Architecture of Ideas'*. I don't think that practicing NLP methods without having a fundamental appreciation of these foundational ideas benefits either the trainer or the practitioner. I invite you to think about these ideas as resources you can use as a conscious change leader to broaden your perceptual map and, thus, increase the range of your behavioural, cognitive, and emotional flexibility.

xviii   *Introduction to the book*

Chapter 7: The NLP paradigm

As with every learning community or community of practice, within NLP circles there is a cultural paradigm which functions as the expressive engine of the community. It guides and enables the value system and, to a large degree, influences how the field will develop. As with all other cultural groups, the NLP community has a shared paradigm that serves as the expressive engine of the NLP world. The early developers of NLP have made these cultural themes explicit through their work, thus revealing the underlying paradigm of NLP. I have selected ten meta-presuppositions that are widely recognized as being at the heart of the NLP cultural paradigm for review. Whilst not all NLP practitioners will follow this paradigm, most will be familiar with its content. The NLP paradigm provides a set of filters through which change leaders may direct their attention inwardly and outwardly and act towards the world in general. In this chapter I will review the NLP paradigm.

Chapter 8: Building the case for change

This chapter will address a significant aspect of change leadership which involves building the case for change. Throughout this chapter I will review NLP analytical models that can support traditional change management tools. The process for building the case for change usually involves analysis of the key change drivers that the organizational leadership has become consciously aware of. This analysis speculates on the influence these change drivers will have upon the organization. The case for change tends to be loosely or tightly built around this analytical process. The major flaw in this process is that it tends to be conducted in isolation by senior managers and can even be what could be described as a desk top exercise. The problem is the lack of direct association with the actual analysis on the part of key stakeholders. The process is too analytical at a level of dissociation. What is required is a counterweight to the dissociated strategic planning tools; NLP provides such a counterweight which will provide the focus of this chapter. The counter-weights are the 'SOAR model' and the 'SCORE model'.

Part 2: Applied NLP

Chapter 9: A model of psychological safety

This chapter explores a model through which change leaders may build a culture of psychological safety through NLP to enable the development of the diffusion model of change leadership. In established management practice, there remains a disproportionate reliance on the transmission model of change leadership fuelling the 'disengagement epidemic'. The ideas that I am advancing regarding what is required to build psychological safety through-out a change management community are not commonplace in the change

Introduction to the book xix

management literature. Psychological safety functions as a sense-making primer which helps the change project attach to the established culture and provide lasting effects and protection from being undermined. NLP methods can function as an enabling technology to apply psychological safety to the established operating culture of the client organization.

Chapter 10: Un-packing the mindset mix

This chapter will define the concept of a mindset. In doing so I will unpack the mix of variables that generate our mindsets. Our mindset shifts throughout the day. In NLP terms, we would call our mindset a nominalization; the conversion of a verb into a noun. There is a tendency to reframe the process of mind that influences our choices of emotional states; cognitive states; and behavioural states, from a process of symbolic interpretation and social construction into a thing, a part of us that is somehow fixed and outside our control. In this chapter I will define mindset as a process, as a verb, that is very much under our control and open to our influence if we can access a meta-reflective state.

Chapter 11: Meta-programmes

This chapter will address the ways in which the mindsets of change leaders can be shaped and changed through adjustments to the meta-programmes they habitually used. The meta-programme we choose influences the nature of the emotional, cognitive, or behavioural state we adopt as a social strategy and these internal strategic decisions have a causal influence on our social results as change leaders. I will employ the NLP model of meta-programme auditing which will help change leaders to recognize un-resourceful meta-programmes and transform these into resourceful states that enable successful change leadership outcomes. I will also examine a technique known as 'perceptual positioning' as a method of calibrating and changing our meta-programmes through a role modelling exercise.

Chapter 12: Framing of experience

This chapter will explore NLP methods for generating ontological flexibility which basically means the ability to hold multiple models of the world simultaneously, to respect and pace the models held by others, and to facilitate a reframing process through which a shared model can be built by the change teams through dialogue that presents a basis for collaboration and action.

Chapter 13: Caretaking and guiding

In this chapter I will address the foundations of a change leader's role which involves caretaking and guiding change participants' experience of the change

xx *Introduction to the book*

work that is to unfold. Guiding involves directing change subjects along a journey of generative change from one state to another, whilst caretaking involves providing a safe and supportive environment for this process to emerge successfully. This means that change leaders must insist that the venues they plan to use as coaching containers are environmentally sound, psychologically safe and have a physical set-up that enables generative dialogue. Change leaders should not perceive these details as pedestrian, or factors that should be addressed by others. Change leaders must be able to meta-reflect on their own states and the energy they are giving off and the generative field around them that they are co-creating with the participants.

Chapter 14: A model of rapport building

This chapter will consider the subject of rapport which is central to NLP practice as well as being the guiding principle for change leadership efforts. Rapport is, arguably, the magical ingredient that is at the base of all successful relationships and, thus, is seen by NLP trainers and practitioners as a vitally important skill. The early developers and pioneers behind the birth of the NLP movement spent considerable time 'modelling' excellent examples of rapport strategies. They modelled the rapport-building skills of world class therapists who achieved consistent success at guiding clients through complex personal and family change. We must reflect on the social strategies we are employing and use the feedback constructively to adopt a different approach to build rapport. This type of thinking is known in organizational studies as reflective practice and NLP practitioners are, by definition, reflective practitioners. In this chapter I will survey NLP techniques and ideas which can enable rapport-building processes to emerge as significant change leadership skill sets.

Chapter 15: Communication models

This chapter will build a model of NLP communication strategies that can enable effective stakeholder engagement during periods of change. A principle of NLP is the idea that 'the meaning given off is the meaning received' which means that we may think we know what we mean when we communicate; however, we don't know what our audience think we meant and how they construct their maps based on our utterances. Thus, we need a model of communication that operates with these facts. NLP provides such a comprehensive model.

Chapter 16: NLP and OD: two not-so-distant relatives. It's time for collaboration

This chapter will compare the genesis of both the NLP and organizational development movement (OD). I will present a picture of the seminal moments that acted as developmental catalysts for the two areas of change work and

Introduction to the book xxi

demonstrate their remarkable similarities. I close by arguing that there is a strategic need for NLP to find a new sponsor to inject vitality and purpose into the field, inclusive of a significant push towards high quality research into its effects as well as aiming towards continued development of its conceptual and practical architectures. The chapter closes with a principle that is common to both NLP and to OD, which is that to be successful as a conscious leader one must model the change one wishes to see in the world.

Part 1

The theory and operational context of NLP

1 Conscious leadership

Introduction

In this chapter I will introduce my definition of the change leader and the specific idea of Conscious Leadership that will form part of the conceptual and practical framework to connect with the overarching themes of the book. I will introduce the practical activity of meta-reflection as a core change leadership capability. I have designed a short reflective statement regarding my own change journey as an explanation regarding the motivations behind this book. This chapter is intended to encourage the emergence of the reflective practitioner that lies within all of us involved in leading change initiatives.

Defining the change leader

The change leader can be understood to be any manager who has been tasked with leading a change project to a successful outcome within an organization. The change leader as a job title is usually implicit rather than explicit. It is normal for the change leader to hold a foundational job title such as HRM manager, operational manager, IT manager, general manager, team leader, or head of department. The secondary title of change leader is rarely written on the person's job description. Rather, it is an implicit expectation that the manager in question will (A) provide leadership to followers when required, and (B) lead their followers through episodes of planned change management interventions on behalf of their employers. The change leader often inhabits two worlds, (1) the world of managing established processes concentrating on making variables predictable and controllable, and (2) the world of unpredictable social outcomes imbedded within change leadership processes. The change leader may, or may not have been formally prepared for their role and therefore may hold impoverished maps in relation to the complicated task of change leadership and thus have fewer options regarding the strategic choices required in terms of behavioural, conceptual, and emotional flexibility.

We need a more specific understanding of the identity of a change leader. The current term is too general, and it implies an external focus where the manager leads others in the execution of their work. When we review the literature on the causes of failure rates associated with change projects, we identify

4   *Conscious leadership*

the emphasis is on weakness in soft leadership skills rather than hard leadership skills (Parkes, 2011; McCalman & Potter, 2015). The latter involves the technical skills associated with an occupation and associated analytical skills. The former involves the inter- and intra-personal skills necessary to build collaborations and dialogues with others. By intra-personal skills I am referring to the capabilities we have for managing our emotions, behaviours and thinking styles and reflecting upon the ways in which these expressions impact on our external relationships. By inter-personnel skills I am referring to the capabilities we must build to maintain open and co-operative relations with others.

The change leader needs to be comfortable with hard analytical change techniques such as 'mapping out change' (McCalman et al., 2016), and the softer cultural side of change which involves managing one's own inner states and building a generative field of dialogical exchanges between stakeholders (Dilts, 2017). This book mainly addresses the latter skill set.

As the world of work changes it is important that those in power who are charged with the strategic development of organizations are equipped to manage both first and second order change. The former deals with incremental changes in established methods, structures, and systems, for example, replacing one IT system with another; the latter deals with the ability of organizational members to critically reflect on the way they do things, why they do things the way they do them and to generate a productive state as a group phenomenon and a critical leadership competency.

Many change leaders are stuck in the 'transmission model' of change management (Alvesson & Sveningsson, 2015) employing broadly transactional methods. This model relies almost exclusively on hierarchal power and reward and punishment systems to motivate change teams. This model, I feel, is outdated and redundant relative to a modern workforce. A cultural shift is required towards the 'diffusion model' embracing coaching and transformational leadership techniques utilizing intrinsic reward systems as key motivators. The diffusion model relies on an approach to change based on principles of organizational democracy and generative collaboration and stakeholder dialogue. The intrinsic rewards are based upon building a shared identity, common and compelling vision, and a shared sense of mission throughout the change network. Anderson and Anderson (2010, p. 3) recognize the need for this and they argue that managers need to *"transform their beliefs about people, organizations, and change itself; they must view transformation through a new set of mental lenses to see the actual dynamics of transformation; and they must alter their leadership style and behaviour to accommodate the unique requirement of transformation."* A conceptual and practical model of change leadership which meets with our requirements is that of 'Conscious Leadership'.

The conscious change leader

Dean and Linda Anderson (2010, p. 3) advance the idea of conscious leadership as an identity construct that I think best fits contemporary change leaders.

Conscious leadership 5

Dean and Linda describe conscious leaders as *"a new breed of leader for a new breed of change"*. They describe conscious leadership as involving *"a required shift in both leaders and consultants consciousness regarding how they view change, themselves, and their roles as Change Leaders."* Conscious change leaders are people who set out to master their own internal resources and the art of change leadership in general. They have a model of human nature, especially motivational drivers, and they understand the butterfly effect, i.e., a slight change in the values, beliefs, cognitions, behaviours, or emotional strategies in a potential leader can and often does create a ripple of change throughout the client's socio/cultural system as others model the new expressions.

Conscious leaders are sensitive to their own inner world views; they are deliberate regarding their choice of social strategies and are habitually self-reflective regarding the feedback they get from social interactions. A key capability of a conscious change leader is the ability to meta-reflect on the part that their emotional, cognitive, and behavioural strategies in use played in generating their social results. Conscious leaders lead their emotional, cognitive, and behavioural strategies; these do not lead them. This means that they are self-disciplined at a level of meta-reflection. They minimize their tendency to react impulsively and unreflectively and they make a real effort to build empathetic competencies and the skills required to understand people. This book aims to share the ideas and skills required to build conscious leadership capabilities. A key conscious leadership skill is that of meta-reflection.

Conscious leadership skills involve mastery of the following variables:

- Mindset: the attitude of mind we construct based upon the way we perceive the world and the meanings we attach to our perceptions.
- Soul: our sense of community purpose and desire to serve and help others be the best version of themselves.
- Ego: our sense of 'I', our individualistic persona, our framework for self-validation.
- Emotions: an affective state of consciousness, instinctive or intuitive feeling towards an object.
- Cognitions: our thinking patterns and preferred sensory system.
- Meta-programmes: our cognitive strategies for interacting with the world to generate our social results.
- Behaviours: the strategies we use to enact our meta-programmes through interactions with our self or with others.
- Values: the scale of importance we place on a social object.
- Beliefs: the principles regarding the world and our experiences that we adhere to that we regard as being true.

All of the above can be regarded as states of being. Anderson and Anderson (2010) describe states of being as *'ways of being'*, and argue that the ability of a person to meta-reflect on their way of being is a critical conscious leadership skill. They define this concept in the following way: *"It (Way of Being) can*

6   *Conscious leadership*

be used to describe how leaders are 'being' and expressing themselves at any point in time or how they are relating to others in various circumstances and situations. While mindset causes emotions and behaviour, the combination is the source of a leader's way of being" (2010, p. 169). For me what is useful about this definition is that it implicitly points internally towards the inner sense-making dynamics of the conscious change leader. I prefer the tag 'state of being' to 'way of being' because it allows me to be very specific regarding the state of being I am meta-reflecting towards. Therefore, throughout this book I will refer to states as social strategies we employ to create our social results. NLP applications are geared towards managing and changing our states of being. The ability to self-calibrate at the level of meta-reflection and change one's state of being if it is not generating resourceful results through NLP applications is the subject of this book.

Meta-reflection

Meta-reflection involves the potential for conscious reflection towards meta-cognition; meta-emoting and meta-behaving. These are all meta NLP techniques that are arguably foundational constructs supporting and underpinning the broader repertoire of NLP patterns and interventions. A NLP pattern is the specific process-led activity that generates changes in our beliefs, attitudes, emotions, behaviours and thinking strategies which results in a shift in our social results. The term 'meta' means something that stands above something else. For example, if one is frustrated at a change management meeting, meta-emoting would involve the process of accessing a state of active curiosity to define the primary state (frustration) and enquire into how resourceful this emotional state of frustration is in this moment. This process of reflexive thinking is also identified as a critical competence for the conscious change leader and, indeed, the general team leader throughout the organizational change literature (Schon, 1984).

The conscious change leader needs to develop their meta-thinking capabilities as a critical tool. To be effective, they need to be able to critically reflect on their emotional, cognitive, and behavioural strategies, and how their choices are influencing their competence as a practitioner. Importantly, the conscious change leader needs to be able to identify the way they are generating their perceptual maps and the processes they employ that delete, distort, and generalize their experiences. The NLP technique developed by Bandler and Grinder (1974) known as 'The Meta-model' which is a set of language-based questions can be used to calibrate one's filters and access deep structure sense making to generate richer and cleaner perceptual understandings or maps. Importantly, for conscious leadership to be authentic it naturally involves the conscious leader being able to honestly reflect on how they lead in practice, not in terms of their ideal socially desirable model but, rather, their model of leadership in practice (Argyris & Schon, 1978).

Conscious leadership 7

A central presupposition that guides the writing throughout this book is that conscious change leaders are fundamentally working within cultural and social systems. The socio/cultural system is dynamic, it is not static. Conscious change leaders have the potential to function as significant others and stand as role-models for desirable capabilities in their organization. Therefore, change leaders are, as Alvesson and Sveningsson (2015) claim, meaning-makers. They are important and active sense-making agents and they do have free agency to change the internal drivers that generate their attitudes, emotions, cognitions, behaviours, and relationships. When they exercise this generative power for personal change they cannot avoid disrupting the wider socio/cultural field that they operate from. Thus, they create the butterfly effect which, taken literally, means that they will stimulate shifts in the meaning systems and related social strategies in others throughout the wider socio/cultural field.

Within the above lies the essence of NLP as a conscious change leadership resource. The changes start from within. If they are perceived to be successful, then the strategies generated by conscious change leaders that produced the results will be unconsciously modelled by their followers. Modelling involves the analysis of the success factors that enable someone or a group to generate success and to adopt these success factors into behavioural, emotive, and cognitive resources to generate similar results. However, the change process must start with the conscious change leader acknowledging their shadow self.

A confession

As a conscious leadership practitioner, I have composed a confessional to demonstrate to the reader a very powerful technique you could employ that will greatly enhance this book as a conscious change leadership toolbox. This technique is known as 'Auto ethnography' which is basically a 'letter to self'. It is a deeply personal account of the challenges associated with change leadership that are part of what Timothy Gallwey (1982) refers to as 'the inner and outer game'.

We all have two models of self that we internalize and which keep us company as we undertake our life's journey. The first is our socially desirable image of self. This is the ideal version of self that we adopt and try to emulate or at least convince others as being the authentic us. This version of self is particularly relevant front stage as we enact the role of professional managers. This version is the one which is seen to be:

- Decisive
- Strong
- Knowledgeable
- Certain
- Stable
- Reliable

8 *Conscious leadership*

The second version of self, which can be described as our shadow self is the private self that we think others cannot see, hear, or feel. This is our authentic self, which is not to say the desirable self is not authentic, rather it can be manufactured for public consumption whereas our shadow self lives inside of us and is arguably incompatible with the image of the socially desirable self-identity that organizations advance as core competencies in change leaders. Our shadow self may include the following characteristics:

- Anxiety
- Self-doubt
- Low self esteem
- Fear of failure
- Fear of criticism
- Low confidence
- Insecurities
- Emotional stress
- Mental stress
- Behavioural stress
- Parts conflicts

We are always in conflict internally with the various parts we associate with our socially desirable self and our shadow self.

My confession has two purposes: (1) to use my own experience as a device to illuminate the focus of change that will be the subject of this book; and, (2) to introduce the colourful conceptual language that forms the discursive space within which NLP operates. In the chapters that follow I shall define all of these terms and locate them for you in their functional context. I took the time to apply myself to decoding NLP language and when you also do this the field will shed its mysticism and be accessible to you in both practical and thoughtful ways

I invite you to think about your own journey as a manager and as a change leader. Write down your own confession, and explore the areas of social interaction that, on reflection, you acknowledge have hindered your ability to build rapport with others. This is the first step to be an authentic conscious change leader.

Origins

My interest in NLP started during my initial management experiences as a much younger self – although I had no idea that I was interested in NLP as I have come to understand it. I experienced management as an incredibly challenging and rewarding occupation. I found the apparently rational side of management which involved planning, labour scheduling, report writing, business planning, and analysis of all kinds of information all very straight-forward. However, when it came to people management, a term I now understand as relationship management which involves building and maintaining rapport, my experience was not so straightforward. Regardless of whether I was dealing with customers, direct reports, colleagues from other departments or line managers, I sometimes struggled in my interpersonal interactions. As I progressed throughout my career I think I improved my relationship management skills. Many relationships became so institutionalized that if I maintained cultural convention and did not stray from this position then, on the surface, relations looked both stable and productive.

The map is not the territory

Through time I developed my own assumptions, beliefs and value system that welded together to form my map of the world. I also developed models of what social experience should look like; sound like; and feel like. These models became ossified as my own mini experiential models which I used to evaluate social experience. Thus, I enriched my map of the world and developed my own idiosyncratic programme of mind, using it to navigate through personal experiences. I judged all social experience against my internal models and maps of what reality should look like. I was not curious in my approach to colleagues; in contrast, I was mainly judgemental. This is not particularly surprising given that a major problem with western management is that we are implicitly trained to judge others. As a result, when my map and associated models were incongruent with those of others I engaged in both implicit and explicit social conflict with this person, or with that person. I attracted people to me whom I felt I had rapport with, and drove away those whom I felt incongruent with.

I justified my entrenched position through a process of honest criticism. I was well-intentioned and everything I did was motivated by positive intentions. The fault generally rested with the other person. It was their world view that was wrong, not mine. They had to change, not me. They lacked this or that personal quality. I did not appreciate the world view of the other and I did not appreciate the fact that they were also coming from a place that they felt was well-intentioned. I would not take personal responsibility for the feedback I was receiving unless it affirmed my world view. Again, I stress the premise that such pathology is not uncommon in managers and it leads to problematic issues when one engages in change management activities.

As I engaged in many mini struggles with those whom I was incongruent with, I played repeatedly the sub-modalities of my experiences and elicited the associated negative emotions which reinforced the incongruent relations I was building around me. I would delete, distort, and generalize empirical experiences to fit with my map, modalities, and models. This process of re-playing the sub-modalities generated not only emotional anguish but I'm sure they expressed themselves through my physical demeanour. I literally became a physical reflection of my state of mind.

I had developed over my lifetime a series of meta-programmes which guided my sense-making processes and forged my perspectives and generated

10 *Conscious leadership*

my social strategies. The problem for me, though, was that I was unaware of the concept of a meta-programme, its influence on my social results and the idea that I could intervene in the subjective process and change the nature and structure of my meta-programmes and, thus, change my social results. I assumed my personality was fixed rather than dynamic and that I could change aspects of it if they were proving to be non-resourceful to me.

For long periods I was not a reflective practitioner and I was oblivious to the sensory systems that people adopted as sense-making devices. I had little appreciation, if any of the kind of predicates people employed through their talk that pointed towards their lead sensory system. As a result, I did not engage in matching or mirroring behavioural or communication strategies that others exhibited to expand my rapport building skills. I did not calibrate well. Subsequently, my skills at both pacing and leading the experience of others were, at best, underdeveloped. I had no concept of modelling effective social strategies demonstrated by others. I was, apparently, a mind reader who could calibrate the symbolic gestures of the other with such high proficiency of sensory acuity that I had no need for the meta-model as a means of accessing the sense making of the other.

I received no training or education regarding these critical leadership skills and I believe this is not an uncommon situation in many management communities. It is simply assumed that we, as managers, possess such skills. This is a presupposition that I suspect is seriously flawed. I failed to appreciate the idea that all people have their own world view that is based upon their personal paradigm or meta-programme; that this meta-programme was constructed of their cultural ecology which consisted of experience filters such as beliefs, assumptions, values and attitudes, and that these filters were bespoke to the individual. It was natural for people to use their filters to distort, generalize and delete experience data as they made sense of the world around them. They used their filters to build and protect their meta-programme and to compose mind maps of the world as they understood it. These maps of the empirical territory they inhabited were, to them, concrete realities and could often be quite different from my own. This was a hard concept to grasp as I, perhaps like many others, had an ethnocentric perspective on things. I rarely adopted the second person position. I was unfamiliar with the NLP technique of perceptual mapping which could have transformed my relationship management skills.

The birth of the reflective practitioner

Was I alone? Was I the only person who had these limiting behavioural competencies? The answer is, emphatically, no, I was not alone. However, I can now recognize my failings. I can now evaluate them and, more importantly, do something about them. This is because I knew something was wrong, I just could not explain it to myself. Thankfully, I was developing self-reflective competencies as I matured, and I knew that I wanted to change, I just did not know how I should go about changing. I do know that my experience is not abnormal. The great Dale Carnegie, who published *How to Win Friends and Influence People*, admits that he wrote the book because he, himself, was so poor at human relationship management and he realized that as far back as 1937 managers were trained on rational management activities but that soft skills, which are a critical component to management practice, were ignored or, even worse, simply assumed to be appropriate. He wrote his book to address this problem.

The wider context

Before I explain how I discovered NLP, what it is and why it was so helpful to me, I would like to consider my confession in a wider context. If there are so many '*how to do*' books on leadership, team building, customer service, motivation, high performing teams, staff engagement, influencing people and a plethora of other human relations books, surely this means that not much has changed in management since the 1930s and many managers struggle to avoid developing some of the bad practices that I recognized in myself. Management, perhaps, is still dominated by the orthodox thinking of Scientific Management. The dominating assumption in the West, perhaps, is that managers are specialists who have the right to manage and they are in their positions as it is assumed that they are subject-matter experts. Managers tend not to operate as generalists anymore. There is a tendency to specialize in some occupational practice or another, say, accountancy, computers, HR, operations, marketing or procurement. Silos develop and organizations become segregated into mini organizations populated with a network of sub-cultures.

A form of expressive hegemony envelopes organizations and mutates into a socially toxic force which inhibits social development and change. It almost strives to remove the essential element of what to be human involves, which is to co-operate with others for the good of the tribe; to find one's authentic voice whilst respecting the voice of the other; to respect one another. Modern organizations have, arguably, morphed into pseudo tribes. They use the language of respect, dialogue, and collaboration as their theory of action but their theory in action often produces a significant mismatch between talk and actual behaviours (Argyris, 2010). What is even more concerning is that these kinds of organizations manage to convince themselves that this kind of psychotic behaviour does not exist, thus confirming organizational psychosis (Merry & Brown, 1987). The people simply suffer and the dysfunctionality that underpins the pseudo tribe continues to develop and dominate.

Since the 1940s well-intentioned behavioural scientists, psychologists and management gurus have collaborated to develop an alternative theory of management practice which confronts Taylorism. For over 70 years extensive research has been applied to industrial settings to unpack human behaviour and to develop models of intervention into management cultures aimed at improving organizational performance. The problem with much of this research and the practical interventionist models that it produced is that it

12 *Conscious leadership*

often avoids naming the real problem. To target organizational performance is to nominalize a noun. Organizations do not have conscious minds and active reflective social identities, yet the literature implicitly treats them this way. As Anderson and Anderson (2010) in their advancement of conscious leadership capabilities for change leaders argue, the focus of attention needs to be sharpened. The focus of attention must start with the individual who is in a position of significant influence. It must start with the manager. The social skills of managers together with the influencing impact of their cultural paradigm and meta-programme determine the kind of organizational culture that is going to manifest. The social skills of managers determine the change management competencies of an organization. This is because, as Dale Carnegie so adequately asserted, if you cannot influence people by appreciating their individual humanity and their peculiar psychology, you cannot run a business successfully over time. This need can be addressed through NLP education, training, and intervention.

Conclusion

The purpose of this chapter has been to offer a model of leadership as a basis for connecting NLP techniques to change leadership processes. I have presented a view that the established model of change leadership based on transmission and transactional systems is outdated and what is required is a cultural shift towards diffusion and systems of intrinsic rewards. The role of the change leader has been defined and the concept of conscious change leadership introduced. The starting point in the development of one's conscious change leadership skills is the ability to meta-reflect and auto ethnographic self-confessions are practical catalysts to aid you on your journey.

References

Alvesson, M. and Sveningsson, S. (2015) *Changing Organizational Culture*, Routledge.
Anderson, D. and Anderson, L. (2010) *Beyond Change Management*, Pfeiffer.
Argyris, C. (2010) *Organizational Traps: Leadership, Culture, Organizational Design*, Oxford University Press.
Argyris, C. and Schon, D. (1978) *Organizational Learning: A Theory of Action Perspective*, Addison–Wesley.
Bandler, R. and Grinder, J. (1974) *The Structure of Magic*, Science and Behaviour Books Inc.
Dilts, B. R. (2017) *Conscious Leadership and Resilience*, Dilts Strategy Group.
Gallwey, W. T. (1982) *The Inner Game of Tennis*, Random House Trade Paperbacks.
McCalman, J. and Potter, D. (2015) *Leading Cultural Change*, Kogan Page.
McCalman, J., Paton, R. and Siebert, S. (2016) *Change Management: A Guide to Effective Implementation*, Sage.
Merry, U. and Brown, G. I. (1987) *The Neurotic Behaviour of Organizations*, gic press.
Parkes, P. (2011) *NLP for Project Managers BCS*, Chartered Institute for IT.
Schon, D. (1984) *The Reflective Practitioner*, Basic Books Inc.

2 NLP as a field of applied sociology

Introduction

In this chapter I will define NLP based on the definitions which I derived from the work of leading NLP developers and creators. There is no fixed definition of NLP as the field holds many different meanings for many different people. Nevertheless, we need a definition that holds true to the originator's intentions and in this chapter, I will offer such a construction. I will briefly survey the historical roots of NLP to provide you with a sense of accessibility to its development as a field of change practice. Finally, I will consider NLP as a distinctive field of applied sociology with powerful complementary synergies with management science being taught in traditional business schools throughout the world.

Definition of NLP

NLP involves critical reflection towards subjective experience to enable social change. O'Connor and Seymour, (1990, p. 3) define NLP as follows: *"NLP deals with the structure of human subjective experience; how we organize what we see, hear and feel, and how we edit and filter the outside world through our senses."* NLP stands for Neuro-Linguistic Programming. NLP, for me, is not an area of scientific enquiry, rather it is an area of social practice. Whilst NLP is heavily influenced by ideas rooted in science, particularly anthropology, linguistics, psychology, psychotherapy, and political science, the field itself is not and never has claimed to be an area of scientific enquiry. NLP is the product of classic sociological and anthropological research. Its aim is to help people achieve greater social results through the conscious management of social construction processes. To understand what NLP is one must appreciate the logic behind its choice of name.

Neuro

The 'Neuro' element signifies the neurological processing within the brain. This is where empirical sense data are processed and sense making occurs. It

14 *NLP as a field of applied sociology*

is within our neurological vaults that our memories are both created and stored, and it is by working with memories that NLP practitioners can alter meaning systems and associated emotional states, social strategies in use and behavioural norms.

For NLP practitioners, the neurological system includes the complete nervous sensory system throughout the body. Thus, we believe that we all have two minds: (1) our cognitive rational mind; and, (2) our physiological mind or our somatic mind. Derks (2005) argues that the cellular structure throughout our body is part of the system we normally call mind. Thus, we have the part of mind contained within the brain and the wider structure of mind, our somatic mind distributed throughout our body. Consequently, NLP practitioners do not interpret the mind and body as two separate systems; rather, we view these as forming an integrated whole, a change in mind-set will influence a systematic change in physiology.

We also hold the view that our neurological system generates energy which influences the nature of the wider social field. Thus, our emotional states are projections of our neurological sense making and they carve themselves symbolically on our bodies, speech patterns and vocal tone. This process is often unconsciously modelled by others who regard us as significant in some way and, through a device we call mirror neurons, a systematic shift in the mental programmes, emotional states and mind-sets in groups can be stimulated.

Linguistic

The 'linguistic' element signifies the important role that language use plays in NLP interventions and in the neurological processes through which reality constructions are formed and laid down in unconscious thought. The anthropologist Mark Pagel (2013) claims that there are over 7,000 active languages being performed at any point throughout the world. This proliferation of languages is evidence of the variety of cultures that also populate our world. We have, as a race, established an awesome meaning system and the main technology for this accomplishment is our spoken language. This is not to detract from written language systems, or body language; it is simply to point towards the overarching significance of linguistic expression as a critical element of reality construction processes.

A significant challenge for change management teams is the process of accepting new linguistic terms into their culture. Often, they filter and even censor the introduction of language that is not already established as part of their normal conceptual structure. This is because language structures our understanding of experience and the kind of reality models we relate to (Spradley, 1979). Language patterns represent organizational culture and culture is normally defended by its members as it has probably served them well and cements established power structures. If, as NLP practitioners, we can create a climate of tolerance towards the introduction of alternative language patterns and linguistic terms, we can alter the structure of experience modelled by people and, thus, shift their attitudes and corresponding social strategies and, therefore, their results.

Programming

It is generally agreed amongst anthropologists that culture can be regarded metaphorically as a kind of software program and the brain a computer (Hofstede, 2010). Each cultural group runs a different cultural software program that produces its expressions and generates its social results. As NLP practitioners, we also acknowledge this metaphor as a very useful way to think about the ways in which people construct social reality in the theatre of their mind. Thus, the programming element of NLP signifies the fundamental idea behind NLP interventions – that we can literally re-programme our minds to construct new or altered meaning systems that lead to changed emotional states, new attitudes, new thoughts, new social strategies, new behavioural norms, and new results. It also stands as a metaphor for the brain, presenting it as a kind of computer that works as a sense-making centre for us as well as a central control system for all our physiological functions. Our brain, as it processes sense data into memories is – according to the implied metaphor – simply being programmed with data and, as with computers, these programs can be edited. It is this idea that provides the clear linkage between NLP and the social sciences, and the theory of social constructivism (Hofstede, 2010).

If you accept the idea that you never have access to reality and if you accept that our filters (beliefs, values, and selective representations) limit our social imprints, then you can also be open to the idea that as social reality and the meanings associated with it are your constructions then you must have the power to change these impressions. Also, as we are always living in the past, i.e., all memory is a picture of a past event, then moving up and down our timeline to re-programme our sensory impressions is also very possible. These observations are the basis of the programming principles that underpin NLP as a field of generative change practices.

Brief history of NLP

NLP is a child of many theoretical parents. It has its roots as a body of knowledge and practice in psychotherapy, sociology, psychology, anthropology, and linguistics. It is a conceptually rich and fascinating area of thought and practice. NLP was established in 1976 as an integrated field of practice and knowledge by three inspirational pioneers: John Grinder, Assistant Professor of Linguistics, University of California; Richard Bandler, a student of psychology at the same university; and Frank Pucelik a Vietnam veteran who was studying at the university. These three NLP developers collaborated to study the work of three outstanding therapists: Fritz Perls, who developed Gestalt Therapy; Virginia Satir, who worked with family dysfunctions; and

16 *NLP as a field of applied sociology*

Milton H. Erickson, who was at that time an internationally established hypnotherapist. Bandler and Grinder were interested in developing a learning approach that they called 'modelling'. The idea that drove their initial enquiries was that experts have patterns or methods that they use to do what they do in the excellent way that they do it. They thought that they could de-code these patterns and use the knowledge to achieve the same results. They were developing a new learning model.

The three NLP pioneers established a network of action learning sets, which included amongst others Robert Dilts and Judith Delozier, to develop their ideas, methods of practice and to test these on each other. They then took their methods out into the field of therapy and business and generated considerable success in achieving personal and group change that had previously been considered as highly challenging. This development period lasted nearly 10 years and is widely regarded as 'First Generation NLP'. Since then, the field has grown to include 'Second and Third Generation NLP'. This book draws on influences across all three developmental stages.

The early NLP development team discovered that whilst Erickson, Satir and Perls were all therapists, they worked with similar ideas yet they used different conceptual language. The NLP pioneers realized that what they were dealing with was a model of social construction. They developed the metaphor that the brain is essentially a computer which is programmed with data collected through our neurological systems and given meaning with the aid of language. This meant for Grinder et al. that if a person is pro-grammed to see the world as they see it then they could also, with the aid of therapeutic intervention, be re-programmed to see the world or aspects of it differently.

Critically, what these modellers were doing was de-coding how these three therapists achieved their results. They paid particular attention to Dr Erickson and studied the micro process he worked with which brought about his results. When asked how he achieved his results Dr Erickson would often say that he did not know the answer to the question. It is often the case that successful people have unconscious competencies that they themselves are unaware of. The modellers studied exactly how Dr Erickson achieved his results and what emerged was a model of rapport building. The ability of Dr Erickson to build rapport with clients enabled him to work in co-operation with them to achieve substantial personal change. NLP, accordingly, is fun-damentally rooted in the practice of modelling excellence in others and teaching this excellence to others.

Grinder et al. also developed a theory of meaning that was previously established in anthropology, sociology and psychology which advocated the view that people act towards things based on the meaning that these things have for them. Thus, if you change the meaning of an attitude object for the person, you can change their behavioural strategies and their emotional states. They developed a body of work that could be used for modelling purposes, or as a learning resource, or as a medium for personal and group change of the transformational kind. Grinder et al., as Californian-based educational pioneers, worked on their ideas together and in 1976 Grinder and Bandler spent a weekend in a log cabin in the hills above Santa Cruz burning through their emerging conceptual framework. They decided to call their product 'NLP' which stood for 'Neuro-Linguistic Programming'.

A successful track record

There has been and continues to be a degree of controversy surrounding NLP. In my experience if you have attended NLP training and applied it as part of your management skills it is self-evident that the techniques work. If, however, you do not attend a NLP training course there is a possibility that you will succumb to the alternative view that NLP is a pseudoscience, that its methods have not been scientifically validated and that the evidence proves that it does not work. These are simply alternative maps. They are different understandings of NLP. As I stated earlier, NLP is concerned with conscious change leadership and social influencing processes. Its aim is to improve one's social skills. And what do we need social skills for? To have influence and to build productive relationships. We want to influence our social outcomes, and this includes how we think, emote, behave, and the kind of social strategies we design and invoke, which all interact to generate our social results. As a practical tool kit there are millions of people throughout the world who would testify to the power of NLP to achieve change at the level of self and in our social results. For me NLP has been and continues to have a transformational influence on the quality of my life and my social results.

NLP is one of the very few disciplines to have practiced change leadership with impressive results at an individual practitioner level over the last 40 years. NLP has an extraordinary level of success in relation to change interventions. When one applies NLP methods introspectively the evidence overwhelmingly points to a very high success rate. Also, when one engages with groups and explores NLP methods the groups tend to enjoy the experience and acknowledge the effectiveness of the applications and their relevance to change leadership situations. I appreciate that these claims are based on anecdotal evidence and for me NLP works as a change technology.

Also, throughout the world there is a network of NLP institutes which have developed sustainable markets that are characterized by repeat business. NLPU, for example, which is run by Robert Dilts at the University of California offers multiple courses on NLP covering Practitioner, Master Practitioner, Trainer, Master Trainer, Success Factor Modelling, Generative Collaboration, Generative Change, Entrepreneurship, Collective Intelligence, Health Interventions and many more NLP inspired courses. NLPU enjoys a global reputation because the methods work. This is also the reason NLP enjoys the current level of expansion throughout the world and, I think, will continue to

18 *NLP as a field of applied sociology*

grow over the next 20 to 30 years. The reason for this is that as a social change technology the methods are effective, and the world needs such technology that can be easily modelled.

NLP is a very rich area of practice which has now migrated into the fields of sport, politics, business, therapy, personal development, education, health, and community social work. The reason that NLP is so versatile across sectors is that it deals with the structure of subjective experience and describes methodologies for changing structures that are inhibiting personal and group development.

NLP has exploded throughout the world and, to date, approximately 40 million people have undergone some kind of direct or indirect NLP training. World-famous life coaches have emerged, such as Tony Robbins and Paul McKenna, who use NLP techniques as the foundations of their business models and products. There is a global structure of NLP institutes that teaches NLP practitioner and master practitioner courses.

NLP is user friendly

The NLP literature is also presented in a user-friendly way that does not alienate those who, perhaps, do not come from an academic background. NLP also offers five levels of service to practitioners:

1 NLP trainers explain the conceptual structure of the ideas underpinning a methodology.
2 NLP trainers demonstrate how to apply the methodology in practice.
3 NLP trainers invite practitioners to practice the methods in a training context.
4 NLP trainers invite practitioners to apply the methods to actual social change situations outside the training rooms.
5 NLP trainers engage in open frame feedback dialogue with practitioners to evaluate their experience of both practice and application.

The important success factor in the NLP model involves practitioners being open to the ideas and methods that underpin the field of NLP and trying out the methods with sincerity and practicing these so that they internalize the methods and associated values of NLP practice and thinking.

Why does NLP work?

NLP works because it deals with subjective experience and, in doing so, it targets social construction processes both internal and external to the self. For example, if I believe that I cannot write and therefore I will never be an author I can, once I recognize this belief as limiting, identify the historical roots of the belief and reframe the meanings associated with its genesis. I can reconstruct my belief and turn it from a limiting construct to an enabling construct and thus change my internal definition of self. I can believe that I can learn to write, and I can create a book and take it to market as a published author. And I am speaking from personal experience. There is a well-established body of literature that has been scientifically addressed and produced around social construction processes (Boje, 1999). These are the processes through which we create culture and make sense of ourselves and others as well as social situations and create the habits of mind, emoting, and behaving that enable us to fit in and function as part of cultural groups. NLP recognizes that as we construct our identities and attitudes, beliefs and values and emotions and cognitions, we can reflectively go back and restructure these if they are proving to be un-resourceful. NLP has developed a series of patterns that we can enact that are designed to activate social construction processes and generate internal change that results in external change and a broader change in our social results.

The strategies that NLP interventions use are usefully described as micro interactive strategies. For example, belief change involves deep introspective thinking and granular interactive strategic manoeuvres at the core of our meaning systems. They are not abstractions from human conduct in the sense that they are essentially things that people do to themselves that create internal and external effects which can have positive outcomes regarding change management situations. NLP is based on techniques that were practiced by some of the world's leading change practitioners who were passionate about enabling positive change in people. These change practitioners worked with individuals and family groups to help them restructure subjective experience so that they may free themselves from limiting beliefs that were damaging their internal and external relationships. Grinder et al. modelled these world class psychotherapists and, in doing so, mapped out the micro strategies they used to achieve their change results.

A new field of applied sociology

The genius of Grinder et al. and their co-developers was that they also developed a sociology for the new field they were to go on to call Neuro-Linguistic Programming, later abbreviated to NLP. Sociology is the study of human social relationships and institutions. Sociology's purpose is to understand how human action and consciousness both shape and are shaped by surrounding cultural and social structures.

Sociology is an exciting and illuminating field of study that analyses and explains important matters in our personal lives, our communities, and the world around us. At the personal level, sociology investigates the social causes and consequences of human interactions. NLP mainly works at the level of the individual although, as discussed previously, as all societies and the organizations that form these societies are part of open systems, then the butterfly effect is always stimulated when change occurs at the micro level of

20 *NLP as a field of applied sociology*

the structure of human relationships. Thus, NLP has the potential to generate macro level change at every level of society.

Another feature of NLP is that it has its own distinctive language for its ideas and practices which define it as a discreet sociology. It is this language and the associated areas of applied practice, i.e., the change strategies that NLP practitioners and trainers use, that defines NLP as a unique discipline of applied social change in relation to other sociological disciplines.

NLP developers, not trainers, are akin to sociologists as they also emphasize the careful gathering and analysis of evidence about social life to develop and enrich our understanding of key social processes. The research methods they use are based on literature reviews and the acute participant observation in the everyday life of individuals and groups. The research methods, theories, and findings of NLP developers who created and continue to add to its sociology yield powerful insights into the social processes shaping human lives and social problems and prospects in the contemporary world. By better understanding those social processes, NLP developers have come to understand more clearly the forces shaping the personal experiences and outcomes of our own lives. The ability to see and understand this connection between broad social forces and personal experiences is a highly practical preparation for living effective and rewarding personal and professional lives in a changing and complex society. The gift of NLP is that, as an area of applied sociology, it has de-mystified complex social processes and presented to the world a portfolio of methods that, with practice, can create profound changes in the nature of our social results.

Those who have been well trained in NLP know how to think critically about human social life, and how to ask important research questions. They know how to design good change interventions at the micro level of individual and group dynamics and how to carefully collect and analyse empirical data, and structure and present their findings back to their clients in highly productive and 'user friendly' ways. NLP developers are like students trained in mainstream sociology and anthropology as they also know how to help others understand the way the social world works and how it might be changed for the better. It is, perhaps, no surprise that Grinder et al. and their team of co-developers were heavily influenced by mainstream ideas rooted in anthropology, sociology, social psychology, linguistics, and psychotherapy. NLP developers have developed distinctive competencies that enable them to think, evaluate, and communicate clearly, creatively, and effectively. These are all abilities that are critical to the practice of change leadership in organizations.

The sociology of NLP offers both a distinctive and enlightening way of seeing and understanding the social world in which we live, and which shapes our lives. As with mainstream sociology the field of NLP looks beyond normal, taken-for-granted views of reality, to provide deeper, more illuminating, and challenging understandings of social life, in particular the social construction processes that people use to form their model of the world. Through its unique blend of transdisciplinary theories, and applied methods, NLP is a discipline that expands our awareness and analysis of the human social relationships, cultures, and institutions that profoundly shape both our lives and human history. Perhaps, though, its unique gift is its ability to change the nature of subjective experiences and thus have an impact on the nature of our social results.

The evolution of business schools

There may be a temptation to dismiss NLP as a serious change management technology specific to management communities on the basis that NLP was forged from within the social sciences. Perhaps many professional managers may feel that sociological ideas and practices are detached from the hard, practical business of leading change in organizations. This would be an understandable point of view albeit a very limiting one. Many business schools throughout the world have members of faculty staff who were either trained in the social sciences before they entered a business academic career or who were influenced by change management literature that takes a socio/ cultural orientation towards change management.

If one surveys mainstream change management literature which is used as part of MBA programmes it does not take long to identify fundamental concepts that have their roots in the social sciences. The seminal work of authors such as Ed Schein on organizational culture; McGregor (1960) and his proposal of 'Theory Y and X'; Blake and Mouton (1966) on high performance organizations and their 'New Management Grid'; Johnson (2000) and his concept of the 'Cultural Web' and strategy work; and the highly influential work of Argyris (1992) on 'Organizational Learning' have all helped shape the curriculum of MBA programmes and all of their ideas are rooted in the social sciences.

MBA programmes are generally accepting the paradigm that organizations are not only economic and technological constructs, they are also social and cultural systems through which economics and technologies are manipulated by social and cultural forces. I take the view that organizations are cultural social constructs as opposed to the idea that has traditionally been floated within business schools that suggests that organizations have a socio/cultural system that is a variable of the organization. Therefore, it appears self-evident to me that if managers are to be effective at leadership then they need to master the craft of building rapport with people using methods shaped by acute insights into cultural, cognitive, and social processes that shape human attitudes and behaviours. NLP does all of this to great effect.

We need more collaborations between managers, consultants, and management practitioners to produce what could usefully be called pracademics which, basically, involves a fusion between the world of research and the world of management practice to both understand organizational dynamics and to develop interventionist methodologies that are research-based, and work as applied to change technologies. NLP offers a practical bridge between

22 *NLP as a field of applied sociology*

academic approaches to understanding organizational behaviour and change practice within the organization.

Concluding thoughts

The field of NLP is a good example of an area of sociological study which embraces the complete research cycle. NLP developers have researched human behaviour to understand and explain how personal change can occur in the assumptions, beliefs, values, attitudes, and associated behaviours in people. NLP is a very user-friendly set of ideas and related methods which are easily modelled by change leaders and highly applicable to change leadership challenges. NLP is, relatively speaking, a new field; it has its own history although its ideas and methods are firmly rooted in traditional sciences such as sociology, anthropology, political science and linguistics and social psychology. NLP is an effective application because it works with the same sociological processes human beings use to construct their models of social reality and their cultures.

References

Argyris, C. (1992) *On Organisational Learning*, Blackwell.
Bandler, R. and Grinder, J. (1974) *The Structure of Magic*, Science and Behaviour Books Inc.
Blake, R. R. and Mouton, J. (1966) *New Managerial Grid*, Gulf Publishing.
Boje, D. (1999) Hegemonic Stories and Encounters between Storytelling Organisations. *Journal of Management Enquiry*, 4: 340–361.
Derks, L. (2005) *Social Panoramas: Changing the Unconscious Landscape with NLP and Psychotherapy*, Crown House Publishing Limited.
Hofstede, G. (2010) *Culture and Organizations: Software of the Mind*, McGraw Hill Books.
Johnson, G. (2000) Strategy through a Cultural Lens. *Management Learning*, 4: 429–452.
McGregor, D. (1960) *The Human Side of Enterprise*, McGraw-Hill.
O'Connor, J. and Seymour, J. (1990) *Introducing NLP Neuro Linguistic Programming*, Mandala.
Pagel, M. (2013) *Wired for Culture*, Penguin.
Spradley, J. (1979) *The Ethnographic Interview*, Wadsworth.

3 New management practices
Paradigm change

Introduction

An underlying presupposition that guides the writing for this book is that the conscious leadership skills managers need to be effective change leaders are often underdeveloped. Conscious leadership skills as catalysts and enablers for the establishment of psychological safety in groups are often ignored as critical training requirements before and during change leadership episodes. This skills deficit leads to fault lines that undermine the potential success of change programmes. This chapter will explore these ideas and identify important issues that conscious change leaders should be aware of. This chapter will also consider the dynamic nature of work and the shift in the cultural profile of both employees and managers. Finally, this chapter will locate NLP as a social change technology with the potential to enable a paradigm shift in management culture towards a model that has a better socio/cultural fit with society at large.

The world of work is changing and we must adapt

Management communities throughout the world's organizations are experiencing a paradigm revolution. Bureaucratic rational management based on legitimate authority to manage has been the traditional management paradigm which supported the established culture of management practice and thinking. This paradigm has served organizations productively since the Industrial Revolution and is arguably now redundant and outdated.

Many years ago, we could depend on regularity of work, steady markets, and sustainable family incomes. This was the world the baby boomers, now referred to as 'Generation X', enjoyed. In this world we worked reasonably hard, tasks were clearly defined thanks to the influence of standardization and established cultures characterized by predictability and stability. Though we went through challenging times in the 1970s, overall, Generation X enjoyed economic boom. Today the security of employment is very fragile. The profile of a typical worker is significantly different today from 50 years ago. The

24 New management practices

nature of work has moved from manufacturing towards a service and knowledge based economy. Education is much more available. A new generation of worker (Generation Y) is graduating to dominate the employment field and displacing Generation X. We need a model of both management and leadership that fits with the demographic shift in the workforce of tomorrow.

As a result of these demographic changes a significant paradigm shift is taking place across the globe regarding the culture of management practice that has dominated organizations for at least the last 80 years (Alvesson & Willmott, 1996). The group of managers whom we can refer to as Generation X are in their autumn years and the next decade will see their retirement. 'Generation Y' or 'Millennials' are now populating the managerial establishment throughout the world. This is a generation born between early 1980s as starting birth years and the mid-1990s to early 2000s as ending birth years. Millennials have a very different outlook towards what work means for them, how they respond to authority and what their values are compared to Generation X. Therefore, the importance of conscious leadership to build rapport with both generations during periods of intense and fast change is of even greater importance to change leaders.

What is equally important is how executive teams understand Millennials and build cultures that facilitate their performance at work in ways that meet their needs. Executives need a different leadership approach, one that does not rely on legitimate authority to plan and direct. They need a new leadership model that is based on cultural sensitivity, high capabilities regarding intra- and inter-personal skills and an ability to build rapport and sustain it throughout the organization at large. Conscious leadership provides such a model.

Unprecedented economic, political, social, and cultural drivers of change have resulted in change leaders in many organizations considering how best to connect with their workforce so that both leaders and workers can cooperate more effectively in integrated ways. They need to share a vision of the future that can only develop from generative dialogue. The paradigm of diffusion change leadership supported by the meta-theme of building psychological safety are central to the emergence of conscious change leadership practices. NLP applications provide the catalysts and enablers to support change leadership mediated through conscious leadership skills.

If one takes a little time to search social media such as LinkedIn, or the websites of industrial giants such as Google it does not take long to find examples of quality research conducted by industry leaders which identifies conscious leadership skills such as managing one's mindset and being sensitive to cultural dynamics as critical competencies for today's change leaders. As Anderson and Anderson (2010, p. 167) state "*Conscious change leaders, because they explore their own internal dynamics, are aware of the influence of their mindset on their perception and consider it in every critical decision or action they take.*"

Major change challenges: the soft stuff is hard

It is generally accepted that the most significant challenges when implementing change projects are soft leadership skills which aim to change mindsets and corporate culture. In our own study of cultural change (McCalman & Potter, 2015), we identified that a lack of soft skills was very problematic for change leaders. The concept of soft skills which is defined as *'personal attributes that enable someone to interact effectively and harmoniously with other people'* are the kind of capabilities that conscious leaders need to nurture in themselves. A good example of innovative research into the soft skills required to lead high performance teams is the Google Aristotle research project.

Google have a market value estimated at $498 billion. They are cited as one of the most innovative companies in the world. They employ super-smart people and each year they receive over one million applications from hopeful candidates. Yet, the smart people at Google worry about their culture; they worry about the atmosphere, or cultural climate that their staff experience each day. They employ 55,000 people all over the world, yet they believe that they can align their staff members' personal mission in life with the greater vision of the company.

They believe in the idea that change starts with the individual, they further believe that the attitudes, values and beliefs that we all hold inside of us can function as 'new behaviour generators' if the proper leadership and team-based culture can be produced. The Google Analytics team decided to study human behaviour within their global community of employees. They wanted to understand the social factors that enabled the development of high per-forming teams. This was not a basic staff survey; this was something very different. This was 'The Aristotle Research Project'.

Project Aristotle aimed to understand the critical success factors that enabled the emergence of the perfect team. The Google Analytics department (HRM) established a multi-disciplinary research team including team leaders, behavioural scientists, anthropologists, analysts, researchers, and operational leaders. The team adopted the following research model:

1   They reviewed 50 years of academic and practitioner leadership literature.
2   They surveyed thousands of 'Googlers' to understand their experience of team working and their motivations.
3   They interviewed hundreds of Google team leaders.
4   They participated in hundreds of Google team meetings as participant observers.
5   They conducted a global network of focus groups.

Overall the Project Aristotle research team invested millions of dollars to build a model of team leadership which would enable the consistent cultural production of high performance teams. The findings were not unique in terms

26 *New management practices*

of established knowledge, what was of immense interest was the scarcity of the model as a standard organizational phenomenon that they identified as generating consistently high performance. This model was the establishment of psychological safety between leaders and their teams.

Psychological safety

Project Aristotle attempted to solve a puzzle that has plagued organizational theorists for decades and, in doing so, they confirmed an important leadership theory. The theory was that leaders in organizations at every level of operation have a primary responsibility (and it is not to manage tasks) to build a climate of psychological safety through which team members could bring their authentic self to work without fear of ridicule, marginalization, or any other form of limiting social behaviours. I would strongly argue that this is a fundamental capability required in order to be an authentic conscious change leader. Google established principles of normative conduct that enabled high performance teams. Many of the principles they diagnosed are the target of change work imbedded in the NLP tool box. The findings were as follows:

- Googlers enjoyed 10 to 15 minutes at the start of each meeting to build rapport within the group and indulge in personal conversations of a light nature.
- Team leaders were sensitive to this need.
- Team leaders placed emphasis on ensuring that all team members were welcomed and included in the group dialogue.
- Team leaders encouraged free expression.
- Googlers felt authentic; they did not need to mask their authentic selves.
- The team leaders calibrated and paced the experiences, behaviours, mental models, and emotions of team members in a balanced and effective way to build rapport.
- The team could connect with each other, with the group and with the vision, ambition, and mission of Google as a company.
- Googlers felt that their work really mattered and that what they were doing could make a difference for good in the world.
- The individuality of each Googler was openly recognized and celebrated by team leaders.
- Googlers wanted respect and a chance to feel recognized.
- Googlers wanted social enablers as leaders not bosses.
- Googlers expected their model of the world to be paced and acknowledged.
- Googlers actively sought opportunities to express their ideas and thoughts.
- Googlers wanted dialogue.
- The group felt psychologically safe, motivated and in a very resourceful state of mind and attributed much of this to the leadership style of their team leader.

The meta-finding of Project Aristotle, implied by the research notes, was that the team leaders could instinctively create what Global NLP developer Dilts (2016) refers to as a 'coaching container', they were able to build psychological safety throughout the team that enabled social risk-taking and the presentation of the authentic self among team members. What is impressive about the findings of Project Aristotle is that the success factors involved in creating psychological safety in a group context were all conscious change leadership skills which belonged to both the 'intra' and the 'inter personal' dimension of social interactions. These soft skills could be clearly identified, and they could be modelled; and NLP training methods are very capable training vehicles to enable a successful modelling process. In future chapters, I will explain just how this modelling process can be conducted.

Core message: 'Conscious change leadership development really does matter'

The core message is that the conscious change leadership capabilities detailed below should be culturally wired into the fabric of a change leadership approach. These skills, as NLP co-developer and pioneer Judith Delozier states, should be imbedded into our muscles. They should become culturally normative and habits of mind. NLP applications provide the methods to enable this inculcation process. The overarching aims should be to work with both change leaders and their teams to do the following:

- Build excellent rapport with individuals and teams.
- Create supportive change networks.
- Model trusting collaborative relationships.
- Widen their leadership choices.
- Communicate with confidence and impact.
- Master their 'inner game'.
- Work with resistance effectively.
- Develop cognitive, behavioural, and emotional flexibility.
- Manage productive meetings.
- Present their case convincingly.
- Manage challenging thinking styles.
- Build an atmosphere of trust.
- Build stakeholder commitment.

The research team at Google called the sum of all the above '*The quest for a culture of psychological safety*'. Google cite Harvard Business School Professor Amy Edmondson who describes psychological safety as "*a shared belief held by members of a team that the team is safe for interpersonal risk-taking*" (1999, p. 354). So, what does a culture of psychological safety look like? Google researchers identified the following success factors:

28　*New management practices*

- Generative dialogue was normal.
- Pacing the experience of others was important.
- Respecting the model of the world of others was valued.
- Conversational turn-taking was to be encouraged.
- Enabling collective intelligence was a key leadership trait.
- Generative collaboration was a critical group dynamic.
- Co-authorship of corporate vision and mission and ambition mattered.
- Bringing one's authentic self to work was essential to a healthy work experience.
- Above average social sensitivity and empathy was a development skill.
- Feeling secure in a group free from fears of censorship or embarrassment was important.
- Speaking up was to be encouraged.

The challenge facing Google was how to build such a culture throughout their organization. They studied examples of such group dynamics that had emerged organically and, using what we call in NLP a modelling approach, they designed an archetype of the perfect team and a supporting development programme and proceeded to implement a cultural shift throughout their organization. They have developed a simple five-point programme which guides their cultural development which could be described as a cultural model that serves the core Google paradigm.

1　**Psychological safety:** Can we take risks in this team without feeling insecure or embarrassed?
2　**Dependability:** Can we count on each other to do high quality work on time?
3　**Structure and clarity:** Are the goals, roles, and execution plans for our team clear?
4　**Meaning of work:** Are we working on something that is personally important for each of us?
5　**Impact of work:** Do we fundamentally believe that the work we're doing matters?

Pulse checks

Google approached their cultural change initiative with a simple yet very powerful strategy; they created a tool called the 'great teams exercise'. This involved:

1　A 10-minute 'pulse-check' on the five dynamics.
2　A report that summarizes how the team is doing.
3　A group 'dialogue circle' to discuss the results.
4　Tailored developmental resources to help teams improve.

To date more than 3,000 Googlers across 300 teams have used this tool. Google employs people analysts to study human behaviour and to build interventions or create social dynamics which enable Googlers to be the best version of themselves and to feel secure in bringing their authentic self to work.

Psychological safety and NLP rapport building methods

This organizational development strategy at Google resonated with me enormously because at the heart of NLP philosophy is the paradigm that advocates the establishment of psychological safety to enable individuals and groups to be the best version of themselves. In NLP terms we refer to this process as building a coaching container (Dilts, 2016). Another reason this idea chimed with me was that I had worked for many years in environments where I did not personally experience this phenomenon. During these difficult periods, I was out of rapport with significant others.

NLP methods are based on the guiding principle of building rapport with clients, of pacing their experience, of matching their model of the world, of remodelling subjective experience in a collaborative way that involves utilizing collective intelligence and enabling generative change. All these practices were at the very heart of the emerging Google paradigm. I think this paradigm is required to enable the diffusion model of change management or leadership (Alvesson & Sveningsson, 2015) and this model, I think, is exemplified by the Google organization. The diffusion model advances the idea of collaboration and dialogue and counterpoints the transmission model which advances the idea of top down leadership based on hierarchical authority to instruct change. The diffusion model should be augmented with conscious change leadership. I believe that the transmission model is now redundant and part of the traditional management paradigm. The diffusion model is very relevant and part of the new management paradigm.

The critical ingredient that made the difference at Google was the degree of active generative rapport that existed between team members and inter-teams. This is the basic starting point of NLP intervention. NLP practitioners, coaches, and trainers believe that without rapport you only have a transactional relationship which can often disable meaningful dialogue and transformational change. I fear that transactional cultures dominate many Western organizations and this, for me and for the staff in these cultures, is a terrible waste. To enable a change in basic assumptions towards diffusion-led leadership cultures led by conscious change leaders who are in balance with both their ego (ambitions) and soul (greater purpose and mission) we need change management technologies that deal with subjective experience, identity work and micro social interactive skills; NLP offers a toolkit ideally suited to these tasks.

Closing comments

It is the ability of conscious change leaders to manage relationships both internal and external to self that will make the difference in future careers.

30 *New management practices*

We have huge demographic shifts to contend with. We have Generation X (born in the 1960s) trying to relate to the work-based expectations of Generation Y (born in the 1980s) and Generation Z (born mid 1990s). So, it is clear that the key to enjoying one's experience of work and leading productive change management situations lies in the quality of one's relationships. And this is where NLP can support change leaders at every level in organizations to build active rapport that leads to productive relationships and a high-performance culture.

Unprecedented economic, political, social, and cultural changes have resulted in senior managers in many organizations debating staff engagement methods and how to connect with their work force so that both leaders and workers can cooperate more effectively in integrated ways. The question should be *'how are they going to build this engagement culture?'* This was the topic tackled by Google as part of their Aristotle research project into what created the perfect team.

Organizations need to build a new cultural paradigm that emphasizes an engagement culture based upon psychological safety. If a management team is stuck in a transmission model of change management this is because of the nature of the paradigm that controls their expressive choices. To move to a new paradigm which supports the alternative change management model of diffusion they need to undertake a change in basic assumptions. This process can occur naturally in an evolutionary sense or it can be accelerated through a direct and managed intervention using NLP technologies, ideally drawing on industrial examples of winning organizations that have made such a shift.

Perhaps if we turn our attention towards alternative places regarding leadership and the role of all stakeholders in collaborating to generate change based upon a climate of psychological safety we may all discover ways to compete with greater success that we can all afford. To do this we need to unpack the social dynamics that produced psychological safety and identify a model of human behaviour that could meet with the requirements of today's organizations, one that is capable of being modelled by team leaders to the wider organization. NLP offers a practical and proven pathway for change leaders that meets with all the above requirements.

References

Alvesson, M. and Willmott, H. (1996) *Making Sense of Management. A Critical Introduction*, Sage.

Alvesson, M. and Sveningsson, S. (2015) *Changing Organizational Culture*, Routledge.

Anderson, D. and Anderson, L. (2010) *Beyond Change Management*, Pfeiffer.

Dilts, B. R. (2016) *Generative Collaboration*, Dilts Strategy Group.

Edmondson, A. (June 1999) Psychological Safety and Learning Behaviour in Work Teams, *Administrative Science Quarterly*, 44(2), pp. 350–383.

McCalman, J. and Potter, D. (2015) *Leading Cultural Change*, Kogan Page.

4 'The map is not the territory'
Reframing change leadership

Introduction

NLP is ideally suited to enabling conscious change leadership because it is broadly based on social construction processes. The philosophy that underpins conscious change leadership is that '*The map is not the territory*' which basically means all our perceptions are simply maps of a potential reality rather than actual reality – and imperfect maps at best. This is known as an interpretivist ontological position. Ontology is defined as the nature of being (Tsoukas & Chia, 2002). The contrast to the interpretivist position is the positivist position which assumes that reality is accessible in an objective sense and can be measured and underlying principles can be identified for analysis (Denzin, 2001). As conscious change leadership involves how one manages one's subjective experience and that of others, an interpretivist approach offers greater flexibility. This is because organizational change works through social construction processes which can be managed more effectively if we have ways of working with our internal representations of reality constructed within the theatre of our minds. This chapter will consider one aspect of conscious change leadership as a process of reconstructing our mental models of the world as we perceive it. NLP as a change technology is ideally suited to support such a project which is called reframing. Throughout this chapter I shall review two models of change leadership: (1) the transmission model; and, (2) the diffusion model. The concept of '*everyday reframing*' as a significant conscious change leadership process will also be examined and connected with NLP applications.

The map is not the territory

My reality model may not reflect your own even when we are talking about the same situation we both experienced. This is because we operate similar perceptual filters but with different selection criteria. We delete, distort, and generalize our experience based on the selection criteria wired into our perceptual filters. Our perceptual filters are the constructs through which sensory

32 'The map is not the territory'

data is sifted and sorted and organized into sense impressions. We filter our empirical experiences through our:

- Values
- Beliefs
- Presuppositions
- Meta-programmes
- Representational systems
- Education
- Culture
- Class
- Gender

If we consider all of the above as kinds of perceptual filters but each one unique in terms of its selection criteria we can understand why often the map is not a shared territory let alone the territory. Consider Table 4.1, which

Table 4.1 Perceptual filter analysis

Perceptual filter	John	Karen	Fatima
Values	On the job learning	Formal learning via a business school	Action learning informed by academic study
Beliefs	People learn on the job not in classrooms	People need structured professional training and management education	People need to learn by doing supported by formal academic study
Presuppositions	Academic learning is a waste of time	Academic study is better than learning operationally	Operational learning and academic learning create a more powerful learning experience
Meta-programmes	Closed mindset	Closed mindset	Growth mindset
Representational system	Visualisation: "Show me how this works"	Kinaesthetic: "Let's build the programme and get a feel for its value"	Audio: "I like the sound of the idea of merging both kinds of learning"
Education	No formal degree. Vocational Qualifications	MBA Education	PhD in Behavioural Science
Class	Working class	Middle class	Middle class
Gender	Male	Female	Female
Ethnic culture	British	German	Arabic

profiles the selection criteria of three members of a management team who are discussing the idea of designing a management development programme.

As the three managers engage in the meeting, everything that is said and expressed will be filtered by each person and the empirical data organized by the criteria unique to each of them; thus, the maps that they create of the meeting, whilst they may have similarities, will also have differences. Often conflict emerges out of these different maps. This is because we literally live in our own subjective bubble, our own model of the world. The following is an excerpt from the creative work by Carlos Castaneda *Tales of Power* (1974, p. 246):

> *Sorcerers say that we are inside a bubble. It is a bubble into which we are placed at the moment of our birth. At first the bubble is open, but then it begins to close until it has sealed us in. That bubble is our perception. We live inside that bubble all of our lives. And what we witness on its round walls is our own reflection.*

Model of the world

A useful way to think about this concept is to consider a typical change management team meeting. Let us say the managing director addresses a group of 20 managers from across the business. The meeting lasts for one hour and the MD speaks for 45 minutes off and on. After the meeting, a team of researchers meet with each participant. They ask each participant for an account of what they heard, saw, and felt about the meeting and the core message imparted by the MD. The chances are that the research team will build models of the meeting content that share similarities and those that contrast sharply. This is because we all create our own models of reality – our own models of the world – that are dependent on our filters. Our filters are our meta-programmes, values, beliefs, relationships, representational systems, gender, class, and personal history, that filter experience and organize the filtered experience into our own unique model of what occurred. Meta-programmes are the thinking strategies we use to guide our interactions with the world around us. They heavily influence our world views. Our representational systems concern which sensory system (visual, auditory, or kinaesthetic) we rely upon the most to make sense of social situations. This concept of perceptual filters obviously has significant implications for the communicating of a change management agenda which involves navigating a cultural landscape made up of multiple subjective bubbles, or world views.

World views

Our world views are our interpretive frames of reference regarding what we assume to be true. Our world views are the individual frames of reference we symbolically construct that combine to form our model of the world. They

34 *'The map is not the territory'*

construct the content of our bubble. Our world views are based upon our beliefs and values and are expressed through our attitudes. For example, if we view the world outside our own country as dangerous and unstable then the likelihood is we will avoid travel abroad. In a change leadership role, if we hold the world view that financial returns only motivate staff then this will significantly influence the kind of culture we promote through the decisions we make.

Our world views are the social constructions we create of social reality. For example, we may build a reality model of what leadership looks like, feels like and, yes, sounds like. We then, at an unconscious level, present ourselves against this reality model and judge others against it. Reality models are very important as they provide ontological stability to social groups and their individual members. However, they can also lead to perceptual, emotional, cognitive, and behavioural inflexibility. NLP is based upon the premise that we can access these reality models at a level of meta-thinking and review their resourcefulness and, when required, change their content and form to adjust their meaning so that we may change our strategies and create different results.

Reframing

An important activity in which NLP practitioners engage is the practice of reframing which is defined by O'Connor and Seymour (1990, p. 127) as follows: *"The meaning of any event depends on the frame you put it in. when you change the frame you also change the meaning"*. Reframing is the magical part of the NLP tool box. This is a truly amazing resource application that can transform the experience of individuals and groups. There are two main reframing strategies in NLP: (1) content reframing; and, (2) context reframing.

Content reframing involves shifting our perspectives regarding the content of a social situation. For example, let us consider a typical change management meeting. The content would involve the activities, ideas, people, aims, and outcomes that are operationalized within the meeting. So, it may be the case that participants see the meeting as a place that stress is generated and additional work is created. Alternatively, an NLP-trained change leader may interpret the content as resources that can help build a coaching container, a space where all participants feel psychologically safe and can be authentic in their interactions.

Context reframing involves shifting our perceptions regarding the operational context that a social situation is occurring within. Context is defined as the circumstances that form the setting for an event, statement, or idea, and in terms of how it can be fully understood. For example, a change management meeting could be framed in terms of context as an event created by senior management to further their own careers. Alternatively, it could be reframed as an event created by the leaders in the organization to enable genuine collaboration across departments to co-create a strategy in response to threats that are important to all stakeholders.

The important issue regarding reframing is that it involves meta-reflecting which simply means being able to consciously reflect on the frame one has created in terms of content and context and how the meanings associated with your frames are influencing your emotional, cognitive, and behavioural states. Meta-reflection involves questioning the resourceful nature of our frames and, if necessary, reframing by re-programming the modality structure of our interpretations: our modality structures.

Reprogramming

NLP practitioners are attached to the idea that we can re-programme our sense impressions that are the basis of our memories; this process involves changing through an editing process the symbolic content and form of our modality structures through targeting their sub-modalities. We can reframe the content and context of our modalities using dimensions such as distance, time, colours, size, locations, sounds, feelings, beliefs, values, and the personal importance we place on the characters or events involved. This process we call programming.

Modalities

Modalities are the primary sense-making systems such as visual, auditory, kinaesthetic, gustatory, olfactory. These modalities are used to gather empirical data or sense impressions, the sum of which we understand to be memories. They are very important as they have meanings attached that we unconsciously assume to be fixed and these meanings drive our attitudes towards things and, thus, our emotional states and social strategies.

Sub-modalities

Modalities have a structural composition. They have sensory characteristics such as: colour, sound, smell, taste, time, location, purpose, characters. These aspects of the modality structure are known as 'sub-modalities'.

Restructuring sub-modalities

As stated above, our meaning system is based upon filtered visual, auditory, olfactory, gustatory, and kinaesthetic experiences that we call sense impressions. These experiences we may consider as symbolic materials that we make sense of and arrange internally to give meaning to our existence. As we are the artists to our meaning systems, i.e., our artistic accomplishments are our modality structures, it follows that as creators of meaning we can intervene retrospectively and reframe the meanings we attach to a previously constructed modality structure. This may involve changing the intensity, character, and form of sub-modalities. This is a very powerful aspect of NLP as it

36 'The map is not the territory'

can be applied to so many aspects of our subjective experience and, thus, impacts considerably the quality of our lives. It follows that if we are experiencing rapport difficulties with someone we dislike then perhaps if we recognize our power to change from dislike to like and thus send out alternative meta-messages to the other this will improve our chances of building positive rapport with this person or with a group. We know that reframing through altering the structure of our modalities works and that it has a longstanding scientific tradition in sociology and anthropology.

Social constructivism

Social constructivism is a theory of sociology that was advanced by Berger and Luckman (1966) with their book *The Social Construction of Reality*. The main premise of the theory is that all reality is a social construction and that we have no objective access to reality due to the limited power of our senses. As all reality is constructed symbolically and as we are essentially meaning-makers we are then all social constructivists. NLP practitioners assume that as we socially construct reality we can deconstruct our constructions and reconstruct our meaning systems. Social constructivism is the basis of explaining the dynamic nature of organizational culture. It also explains why reframing, as a NLP technique, works so effectively. It is important to internalize the idea that what we put inside our subjective bubble is our creation, our meaning systems, and thus what we socially create in terms of frames of reality we can deconstruct and change, if we choose to.

The leadership challenge: ethnocentric map making

One of the main challenges facing organizational leaders of change projects is the established paradigm of transmission as the core model managers use to advance change in their organizations. This model involves managers designing ethnocentric maps that they then try to impose on others with disregard for their own maps. This is ethnocentric in nature because the manager operates solely from the first perceptual position which is their own model of the world, from their own subjective bubble. Conscious change leaders, in contrast, break free from their first perceptual position and enter the second perceptual position to understand other people's maps. In doing so they obtain far richer perceptual maps, which gives them greater behavioural, cognitive, and emotional flexibility as change leaders. It makes sense that managers who set out to advance their ethnocentric map as the only map are operating from an impoverished position and research indicates that this strategy produces weakness in the stakeholder collaboration and commitment to the overarching change agenda.

The transmission model of change leadership advocates the idea that change management is a rational, even intellectual, activity that simply needs the effective transmission of legitimate authority throughout the organizational

'The map is not the territory' 37

structure for change to happen. This is a very flawed model and, arguably, somewhat discredited in critical management journals. The transmission model is arguably based upon a positivist philosophy. It is a clear case of one group, or one person, attempting to force their model of the world onto others. We know that when the wider majority is excluded from the diagnostic stage of change management, i.e. map making, they tend to disengage with the case for change and retreat into the comfort of their own reality bubble. This process of ontological alienation emerges as a serious case of resistance and blocks dialogue and the development of collaboration based on mutually inclusive maps.

The dominance of established '*How to achieve successful change*' articles and books, which are mainly based on the transmission model, prevent a change in basic assumptions emerging throughout organizations towards an alternative change leadership model we call diffusion. The diffusion model is based on the idea that change strategies should be based on collaboration, enabling collective intelligence, aligning identification processes and active generative and authentic dialogue. This process requires collective map making and it involves conscious change leaders functioning as meaning-makers or, rather, meaning-brokers based on NLP methods such as pacing experience, matching experience, eliciting resourceful states, calibrating states in action and leading sense-making processes as meaning-brokers. Thus, what we need are tools that can enable a shift in the mindset of both managers and change teams to embrace the effective model of diffusion and relinquish the flawed model of transmission. The first important tool is appreciating the principle of '*the map is not the territory*'.

Eminent academics who produce excellent insights for practical managers are Alvesson and Sveningsson (2016) who are experts regarding cultural change issues facing managers in the world today. These two scholars have studied longitudinal cultural change programmes in detail by participating in the cultural processes and studying change close-up. They are particularly sensitive to the way language patterns frame everyday reality for organizational members. Their findings are illuminating and, below, I have listed the top 12 fault lines that they have identified that can undermine, to various degrees, sincere cultural change efforts.

1 Lack of generative dialogue
2 Mismatch between rhetoric and action
3 Limited collaboration
4 Limited role models
5 No acknowledgement of other world views
6 Limited rapport-building skills
7 No construction of a shared vision
8 No construction of a shared mission
9 Weak diffusion of the case for change
10 Lack of vitality in the social system

38 'The map is not the territory'

11 Closed mindset regarding new ideas
12 Top down design processes

It is clear from their critical research that the compounding effect of these factors creates an organizational mindset that disables well intentioned change efforts. My argument is that it is ethnocentric practices within management communities involving efforts to dominate the subjective map-making process and produce models of the world that are to dominate all competing models on the part of the elite that creates many of the fault lines identified above. If we adopt the interpretivist paradigm, respect the model of the world held by others, aim to generate dialogue through conscious change leaderships and encourage collective map-making horizontally and vertically throughout the organization, then the case and motivation for change will diffuse throughout the social system and provide a solid basis for collective action.

One could argue that Western management communities have adopted an orientation from classic management thinking that orientates them towards a paternalistic leadership style or towards the identity of benevolent autocrats. These two identities are synonymous with the transmission model of change leadership. The assumption which underpins these identities is that managers are somehow better at problem solving and identifying flaws in organizational performance that need to be corrected. This assumption is so deeply imbedded in management thought that they would generally be unaware at a conscious level that they think this way. However, if we study managers at work what we often see is that they demonstrate the influence of this assumption through the ways in which they give feedback. They are programmed to see the flaws, point these out and prescribe corrective actions. To make sure that they do this they are also emotionally attached to such social strategies as their identities as managers are inexplicably connected to the performance of issuing corrective guidance. This strategy is effective and has served management communities well over the last 100 years. However, we live in different times and, as Google have identified, we need different leadership traits and tactics which are more appealing to group formation and enabling towards generative dialogue and collaborative working.

It is, unfortunately, the case in many organizations that relationships are impaired by the totalizing influence of hierarchical structures and the pursuit of power and influence throughout the organization. One could define organizations as *'Sites of contested meaning'* through which people compete to be heard and for influence and power. The source of these tensions is the struggle for recognition. Also, the transmission model is based on the allegedly smart people doing the strategic thinking for the rest of the people and then simply transmitting their ideas throughout the organizational structure and expecting things to happen. This model encourages monologue and passive audiences. It also very much reinforces the feeling throughout that psychological safety is not present and silence is a safe tactic. The diffusion model, in contrast, does the opposite; it encourages dialogue and highly participative audiences in the strategic sense-making of the organization. NLP technologies and philosophies such as reframing can disrupt the orthodox transmission model and enable the introduction of the diffusion model of change leadership.

Concluding thoughts

In this chapter I have argued that we all create and hold onto our own personal subjective maps of the world. These maps are based upon our perceptual filters which delete, distort, and generalize reality. All our filters have unconscious bias built into their functionality. A common mistake that plagues management teams and affects change leadership outcomes is the practice of ethnocentric map making and efforts of imposing, unreflectively, our maps of reality onto others. This is an act of applied domination and often leads to conflict and tension in the workplace. Social constructivism, which is an accepted field of scientific enquiry and theory, is the main theory and practical model that NLP practitioners refer to as change agents. The fact that we actively socially construct our maps and if we can acknowledge the maps of others and develop our skills as critical thinkers we will access far greater behavioural, cognitive and emotional flexibility and be able to match and pace stakeholders more effectively leading to greater rapport and the lowering of conflict and tension. NLP provides the habits of mind that can greatly enable this dialogical process.

References

Alvesson, M. and Sveningsson, S. (2016) *Changing Organizational Culture*, Routledge.
Berger, P. and Luckmann, T. (1966) *The Social Construction of Reality*, Penguin.
Castaneda, C. (1974) *Tales of Power*, Touchstone.
Denzin, N. (2001) *Interpretive Interactionism*, Sage.
O'Connor, J. and Seymour, J. (1990) *Introducing NLP Neuro Linguistic Programming*, Mandala.
Tsoukas, H. and Chia, R. (2002) On Organisational Becoming, Rethinking Organisational Change. *Organisation Science*, 13: 567–585.

5 It starts with oneself
The butterfly effect

Introduction

In this chapter I will consider the deeply personal nature of NLP and argue that all changes in behaviours or values and beliefs within an organization start with the self. Organizations are socio-cultural systems and are characterized by the butterfly effect which dictates that a change in one part of the system will result in a vibration throughout the culture that creates systematic change. NLP is a valuable personal development toolkit as well as a resource to enable broader behavioural change. This chapter will also consider unconscious and conscious modelling as a transmission strategy for inculcating preferred leadership styles throughout an organization. I will take our preferred leadership style, conscious change leadership, as the working model and explain how this can be taught at both conscious and unconscious levels of learning to others throughout the organization.

The butterfly effect

The butterfly effect is rooted in Systems Theory and was originally applied to explain systematic changes in weather conditions by the scientist Edward Lorenz. The idea is powerfully simple and can be applied to behavioural and cultural change thinking and practices. The premise of the idea is that there is the implicit promise of group and society change through the concept of the butterfly effect. The basic principle is that any change in the composition of a system will result in wider change throughout the whole system. If I change my values or beliefs and social strategies then you may choose to consciously or unconsciously model and internalize these changes and, thus, we have group change. To be an effective conscious change leader, I must be the change I want to see in the world. I must model the changes I want to see in others with integrity and authenticity. It is this capacity for modelling behaviour that is relative to all human cultures that enables the butterfly effect in the context of organizational change.

If we accept the idea that people are natural modellers, that they instinctively model the behavioural, cognitive, and emotional strategies that they perceive to be socially desirable, and/or are successful at generating desired results, then we can also accept that as conscious change leaders what we believe in and value really does matter. Our beliefs and values are the batteries behind our behavioural, cognitive, and emotional strategies and, as such, they are evident to others. Our expressions reveal our beliefs and our values. What we do reveals what we value and believe in. In change leadership terms this principle cannot be overstressed. If your change leaders start to act as conscious change leaders and create micro changes in their presentation of self, rooted in a shift in form and content of their values and beliefs, you will stimulate the butterfly effect. Assuming the potential role models sustain the changes and inculcate these into their cultural habitus, and assuming they stand as significant others in their organizational culture, then there is a likelihood that all or part of their new habitus will be adopted consciously or unconsciously by the generalized others throughout the organization.

The theory is that throughout the cultural landscape of the organization there is a network of cultural domains, pockets of localized culture where the various managers and team leaders practice their craft as leaders. Within these cultural domains there will be active leadership/follower relations of various qualities being enacted daily. As the butterfly effect ripples through the cultural fabric of the organization, the modellers become cultural carriers of the new value, beliefs and associated behavioural, emotional, and cognitive strategies. This network of cultural carriers can be understood to be culturally contagious and the new leadership model will spread organically and, through time, become established as a cultural norm. This is the butterfly effect.

NLP concentrates on micro strategies aimed at creating sustainable changes in one's leadership or management style. Yes, there is always the idea that as an individual making a difference in terms of established cultural norms it is very difficult to achieve. However, if you assume the philosophy implicit in the butterfly effect you can and will generate changes in the cultural habitus of others and you will create a ripple effect throughout your organization; even if the ripple effect is minute, it has the potential to graft onto the established culture and grow rapidly as a new and dynamic leadership culture. NLP methods are ideally suited to enabling this process of cultural change in an organization. One additional principle or belief that you will need in order to adopt the butterfly effect as a philosophy of behavioural and cultural change is that we are all integral elements of a complicated social and cultural system.

Individual or Holon?

A conversation that needs to be conducted in an organization facing pressure to change, and possibly change rapidly, concerns the ways in which managers and staff perceive themselves. Do they think of themselves as individuals separate from the overarching cultural and social system; or do they see themselves as integrated social beings that are part of an organic and dynamic socio/cultural system that they have considerable influence over? The answers to these questions are of strategic importance to change leaders. This question explores identity: specifically, the two mutually inclusive identities of '*ego*' and '*soul*'.

A significant skillset characteristic of an authentic conscious change leader is the ability to perceive themselves as a Holon (Dilts, 2016), as a part of a broader social and cultural system, and to have a strong sense of soul, an orientation towards serving others and facilitating their development. Ego involves motivational drivers that focus upon self gratification whilst Soul involves serving others; ego motivates individualism ,whilst soul motivates tribalism. Maslow (1943) perceptively identified the idea of a '*Hierarchy of motivational needs*' that is arguably universal across the world's cultures.

Maslow recognized that we have safety and physiological needs at our basic core. These are the needs that 'benevolent autocrats' can satisfy that are traditionally associated with transactional leadership which is not normally aligned with the idea of conscious change leadership. Then, we have higher needs such as a need to be recognized and to self-actualize to develop as part of a group. These needs are normally associated with transformational leaders who are orientated towards a conscious leadership and a diffusion approach to change management , which involves generative dialogue and participative leadership as cultural norms. Conscious change leaders have developed the capability to minimize the constraining influence of their ego which privileges their own perspectives.

Anderson and Anderson (2010) develop a useful model of ego. The ego, according to the authors, involves the socially desirable and insecure version

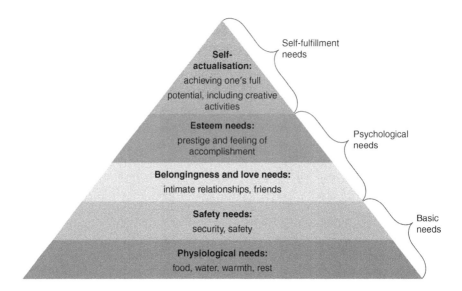

Figure 5.1 Maslow's hierarchy of motivational needs

It starts with oneself 43

of the self, operating instinctively in the world. The ego is our identity as we would like to believe it. Our ego is made up of our socially constructed beliefs, values, and meta-programmes. We use our ego to gain our sense of individuality and it is against our ego that many of our decisions are made. If we are imbedded in an ego state then, arguably, we will also be entrenched in our first perceptual position, be heavily invested in our own ethnocentric maps, and have low tolerance towards other people's maps.

The challenge with the ego is that its primary purpose is to protect us from failure, to separate us from 'them', or the 'other', to give us ontological certainty. Our ego can be considered as our auto pilot, that helps us navigate social dynamics, often unreflectively and in most cases unconsciously. This means that we can lose our powers of empathy and restrict our emotional intelligence development and, finally, minimize the power of our conscious change leadership skills. This is all bad news for organizations involved in leading change when major blockers include fixed mindsets, organizational culture and highly ingrained defensive routines aiming to maintain the status quo. As we develop from childhood to adulthood we become socially conditioned and programmed to unreflectively be led by our ego.

However, we can control our ego and limit its power of mastery over us and enter a state of conscious leadership. This involves recognizing what Anderson et al (2010) refer to as 'our higher being'. For me this is the window into my unconscious mind and I can view from a position of a meta-state the programmes I am running that are generating my emotions, thinking strategies, behaviours, and attitudes that are producing my social results and fuelling my ego. In NLP circles we call this process meta-reflection. Meta means above or beyond something. What we do when entering a state of meta-reflection is we create an internal mentor and we build rapport with this resource. Our internal mentor is the inner voice that we all have chattering away in the background. The value of this strategy is that our internal mentor can move into a meta-state for us and disassociate with our primary emotional, cognitive, and behavioural states and critically examine the resourceful nature of the meta-programmes that are generating these primary states. Our internal mentor can challenge the controlling power our ego has over us from a safe place. Our internal mentor can enable the emergence of our soul as a counterpoint and regulator of our ego.

In NLP terms, our soul is not a kind of spiritual entity. Rather, our soul is that aspect of our unconscious mind that connects our desires and motivations to serving others; to being curious about other people, their culture, world views, values, and beliefs. When we are in a good state of rapport with our soul we are both internally and externally focused. We are in touch with our own world views, beliefs, values, emotions and meta-programmes and we can empathize with the internal representations that others create that generate their maps of the world as they see it. We are in a generative state, an internal state that generates resourceful strategies that resonate with the

44 *It starts with oneself*

people around us and establish opportunities for collaborative action and dialogue.

I am not saying that having an ego is a bad idea. Rather, what I am advancing is the premise that we need a relationship between our ego and our soul that is evenly balanced if we are to operate as effective conscious change leaders. We need to identify ourselves as Holon's, as part of a broader integrated system, who can act as role model for others in the organization at both an unconscious and conscious level of active modelling. We can use the NLP method of meta-reflection to maintain a balanced relationship between our ego and our soul.

If we use the technique of meta-reflection we can self-calibrate how our relationship between ego and soul is influencing our emotional states, thinking strategies, and behavioural norms and question the resourceful nature of these in relation to the change programme and the kind of productive and collaborative relationship we are trying to build with the change teams. Anderson and Anderson (2010), in their work on change management, refer to this process of internal state management as basically constituting conscious change leadership.

Anderson and Anderson (2010) also argue that a major problem with many change leadership projects is that the senior team are in autopilot mode. This is an unreflective action orientation relying on instinctive retrieval of models of management that worked previously. This may be an effective strategy when dealing with either developmental change or transitional change, but not so when dealing with transformational change. In fact, it is probably a weak strategy for managing developmental and transitional change projects also. This is because the effect that one is having on team members is not being critically assessed by the leader and, thus, problems can be created that could be avoided if the leader applied conscious leadership via meta-reflecting to carry out their duties.

Once, a very experienced HRM executive at the end of an NLP course turned to me and asked "*David, I understand how this NLP would be helpful to me in terms of my own issues, though I am struggling to understand how we would use it to sort out... well... the prickly customers we have to deal with.*" I think this, at one level, was a reasonable question though it also struck me as evidence that they had missed the point of the course. To change a cultural system, one must make changes in one's own internal cultural system, meta-programmes of the mind, attitudes, and social skills, if one has any chance of stimulating change in others. One of the significant advantages of NLP is that one can apply many of its strategies to one's self. To emerge as a capable conscious change leader, one needs to be able to morph into a Holon, appreciate and value your being as existing in a cultural and social system that rewards you if you feed it. This involves us committing to the idea of service; we are, by nature, leaders only if we have followers and followers choose their leaders based on how best they serve their interests. To establish a culture of conscious

It starts with oneself 45

change leadership one needs role models and an understanding of modelling processes.

Modelling

Modelling involves internalizing as a habit of mind the cognitive, behavioural, and the emotional strategies that another person uses to generate a social result. Dilts (1998, p. 29) defines 'modelling' as *"involving observing and mapping the successful processes which underlie an exceptional performance of some type. It is the process of taking a complex event or series of events and breaking it into small enough chunks so that it can be recapitulated in some way."* Dilts (1998, p. 29) explains that the purpose of modelling is to *"create a pragmatic map or model of that behaviour which can be used to reproduce or stimulate some aspect of that performance by anyone who is motivated to do so."* Bearing in mind that the purpose of culture is to gain control over one's environment so that the group may be successful, then it is logical to assume that if a leadership style is seen to be successful others will unconsciously model the success factors that generate the leadership style and its social results.

Modelling was the original intention of Bandler and Grinder (1975) as pioneers of NLP. The principles of modelling are that:

- All excellent behaviour can be considered as a social strategy.
- Social strategies can be process mapped.
- Each element of the strategic process can be modelled.
- Social strategies once process mapped are known as patterns.
- We can imprint ourselves into the psychology of the performer we wish to model.
- We can focus on what the performer does and how and why they do it.
- We can isolate the discreet parts of the pattern for study and understanding.
- We can delete parts that do not have much influence on the outcome.
- Thus, we can re-engineer a pattern for accelerated learning.
- We can design teaching strategies so that others can learn the pattern.

Modelling is not always done at a conscious level. We are all culturally wired to unconsciously model excellent social strategies demonstrated by significant others in our experiences. The most powerful example is that of modelling habitus which is defined as the manners, ways of speech, accents and physical expressions adopted by a member of a particular class. As a child matures, it models the habitus of its parents and, thus, reproduces the identity culture of the class from which it originates. This is a good example of unconscious modelling. In corporate settings, leadership styles associated with significant others may be modelled unconsciously by those who aspire to similar leadership positions. The power of NLP modelling is that one's

46 *It starts with oneself*

modelling capabilities are greatly enhanced when one becomes unconsciously competent at the modelling process through study at a conscious level of modelling processes. Reflective practice makes perfect practice.

Anthropology as a source of modelling catalysts

There is no doubt that to change a leadership culture we need to use proven methods. Within anthropology we have the basis for a very successful cultural change intervention regarding the leadership style associated with a cultural group. This resource can be usefully described as modelling catalysts which are defined as cultural processes which enable the modelling and inculcation of behavioural, cognitive, and emotional strategies imbedded in a sense of identity that is approved of within the culture. We know that anthropologists have studied the sense-making process, rituals, routines, stories, values, and beliefs that generate cultural themes that guide the expressive choices and capacities of cultural members. And we know that they, in partnership with sociologists and psychologists, have identified the micro processes or strategies people use at an unconscious level of thought to model cultural norms. There are three modelling catalysts that we use in NLP to enable successful modelling.

Mirror neurons

A mirror neuron is a neuron that stimulates the matching of a behavioural, cognitive, or emotional state being projected by a significant other (Hatfield et al., 2014). The neuron mirrors the behaviour of the other, as though the observer were themselves acting. If a leader adopts a critical mindset towards a change programme, then there is a strong possibility that their followers will match their mindset and even the corresponding emotional state and behavioural model. The stimulant for this is the firing of the mirror neuron. The mirror neuron will only be activated if the role-model is regarded as a significant other by the observer and their peers. The peer group is 'the generalized other' which has considerable influence over the sense-making processes of its members. If the generalized other subjectively interprets an individual as a 'significant other' then there is a high probability that they may model aspects of the significant other's world view and social strategies at the level of cognition, emoting, and behaving. As stated earlier, this process of modelling will also involve the values and beliefs of the significant other.

Matching

Matching as a modelling catalyst involves adopting similar cultural attributes to the other such as:

- Body posture
- Voice tone; and speed
- Emotional states
- Meta-programmes

It starts with oneself 47

- Preferred representational systems
- Beliefs
- Values
- Behavioural strategies
- Clothing style
- World view

Matching is defined at one level by Dilts and Delozier (2000, p. 698) as: *"The process of reflecting or feeding back the cognitive or behavioural patterns of another person."* If you do this effectively you will act as an unconscious mirror to the other who is more likely to relax with you and enter a state of dialogue. Matching is a fundamental process which is essential to building and maintaining and developing a culture. When we are infants we unconsciously match and, thus, model the culture of our parents which includes language, customs, and behavioural norms. It appears that human beings are culturally wired to respond favourably to matching and that it is fundamental to cultural change processes. Moving from a transactional leadership culture to a transformational leadership culture characterized by conscious change leadership traits would require active modelling and acute matching throughout the cultural group involved. It is difficult to conceive of a culture that does not, at the level of a critical mass, share many of the above cultural attributes. Thus, matching is a very important modelling catalyst.

Anchoring

Anchoring is a modelling catalyst; it enables us to deeply imbed the cultural traits we want to model into our unconscious mind so that they become part of our cultural habitus. Dilts and Delozier (2000, p. 29) define anchoring as *"The process of associating an internal response with some environmental or mental trigger, so that the response may be quickly, and sometimes covertly, re-accessed."*

Anchoring, involves directly associating an experience with a core symbol. For example, the act of prayer is an anchor as the ritual directly associates the person praying with their religious belief system and fires the state of faith. All cultures are founded upon a system of anchors which may be in the form of material symbols, or they may be imbedded in language activated through rituals and routines, or they may be more abstract rooted in ideas or beliefs. What the pioneers of NLP did was to use the idea of anchoring as a modelling catalyst. If you wish to model a conscious change leader's cultural trait then you would directly associate with their model of the world and anchor the state of mind this generates in you.

The anchoring process, when it occurs organically, is arbitrary. However, change leaders trained in NLP can purposefully set up an anchor in the mind of a change audience. For example, they can use change mantras repeatedly to anchor ideas and belief systems to experiential reference points. A change mantra is a short sentence that contains anchors relating to an outcome. Examples of change mantras that contain anchors would be:

- "We are all in this together."
- "If we don't change our jobs are at risk."

48　*It starts with oneself*

- "We are stronger together."
- "We must be competitive to retain and win customers."
- "It is the quality of your work that will determine job security."
- "Together we can build our shared circle of success."
- "Our vision is a winning team."

The choice of words is evocative and intended to stir internal representations in an audience's mind and trigger specific emotional states. The organization can then design marketing images around these verbal mantras that visualize the empirical context.

Unconscious modelling

We can use success factor modelling techniques as analytical tools (Dilts, 2016) to unpack the cultural traits that sustain a model of leadership in a significant other. Then we can develop training programmes based on modelling principles to inculcate our management community regarding the conscious change leadership model we are advancing. However, we can also encourage unconscious modelling based on organic sense-making processes.

When people start to unconsciously model the cultural traits of someone in the workplace what they are doing is signifying their acceptance of this person both as a role model and as a leader. Let us consider the following example.

John was the management accountant for an IT business located in London. John worked for an organisation whose managing director had a reputation for a very laid-back leadership style. The MD loathed confrontation. She placed emphasis upon maintaining good relationships. She was a master at impression management. She instinctively paced the experience of others and never revealed her inner thoughts regarding any subject. She would never contradict a speaker, or interrupt their flow. When dealing with key stakeholders she would keep the conversation very light and steer away from topical issues that may present tension points. She was very active in the local charity that's served her business offering scholarships to emerging industry talent and was an active golfer. Her overarching philosophy was overt delegation and she never intervened in her team's activities. She was very popular and, as a figurehead, represented the organisation extremely well and professionally.

John, whilst having achieved his accountancy qualification and a degree in business studies in his younger life had, basically, avoided any executive management education throughout his career. He found himself working directly for the MD. Through time John started to unconsciously model the traits that the MD demonstrated as consistent features of his social strategies. He developed a pathological defence against revealing his inner thoughts. He applied himself diligently to serving the charity that his boss had set up. He enthusiastically practiced and participated in golf outings

It starts with oneself 49

> with his boss and the broader stakeholder network. He avoided confrontation and adopted the '*Three Wise Monkeys*' philosophy of '*see no evil; hear no evil; speak no evil*'. He never challenged his colleagues or intervened in any of their activities or voiced an opinion regarding what they could be doing to make the business stronger. He was eventually appointed via corporate coronation as the new MD when his boss retired.

We would need to take some time unpacking the success factors that enabled John to be perceived as the natural successor to the MD. However, what we can see at a glance is that it is highly probable that John was successful because he mirrored the leadership model that his MD was operating through. He may have done this at a conscious level of social strategizing, though this is not that probable. It is more likely that he simply unconsciously modelled his MD because his meta-programme was strongly orientated towards matching and away from mismatching. He had an ability to hold onto difficult feelings and not reveal these, to build connections with his MD and build rapport that smoothed their working relationship. He was a talented modeller. If he had a different MD with a very different cultural profile in terms of leadership traits I think the likelihood is that John would have modelled this just as effectively. The challenge for John, and for his colleagues, is authenticity. Does he have an authentic model of the world that leans towards behavioural, cognitive, and emotional flexibility that is generative in the absence of a role-model, a significant other? If you formally teach John how to model and how to meta-reflect then I think he would self-generate the behavioural, emotional, and cognitive flexibility he requires to adapt to a given situation. If he did not have a role-model in his social space, then he would simply reach out beyond his comfort zone and locate one. This kind of reflective awareness is essentially what is involved with conscious leadership skills.

There is much we can learn from other disciplines such as anthropology, psychology, sociology, and systems theory to help us be far more effective conscious change leaders. There is a compelling case for the fusion of theory and practice and to encourage the cross fertilization of ideas if organizations are to balance their ego culture with their soul culture. Dilts (2016) argues for the ideal organization that is characterized by a culture of conscious change leadership through which the ego and soul, as collective subjective entities, are held as generative and complementary which enable ambitions to be pursued whilst maintaining a healthy commitment to a broader sense of mission based on a vision of a world that organizations want to live in.

In my experience, a common mistake that potential leaders make is to assume that they, on their own, cannot change the culture they work through. This is both a leadership failure and the philosophy of an individual, not of a Holon. Through NLP we can loosen such limiting beliefs and encourage and facilitate the acknowledgement of each person being a Holon and of their power to activate the butterfly effect throughout the organization. This, of

50 *It starts with oneself*

course, depends on each person identifying with the overarching systems and taking responsibility for the part they play in sustaining established cultural norms that privilege ego over soul, individualism over holarchy, and ambition over vision. The ideal scenario is a heathy equilibrium between these forces; as they are not necessarily mutually exclusive they can be mutually inclusive and establish what Dilts (2016) calls '*The circle of success*' that unites all stakeholders behind the strategic change agenda for the organization.

Concluding thoughts

NLP is based upon the principle of systems thinking and the meta-idea that as we are all individuals and Holons that connect to a broader holarchy or cultural system, when we make changes in ourselves at the level of cognition, emoting and behaving we can stimulate changes in our broader cultural system. By taking responsibility for our social results we can use these as feedback mechanisms to refine or transform our social strategies through modelling processes and, thus, change the nature of our social results. The argument that states that culture cannot be changed, or if it can it is incredibly difficult to do so, is a limiting belief. All individuals have the power to model new behaviours, values and emotions and this modelling process can and does trigger broader cultural change through the butterfly effect. Once our basic motivational drivers are satisfied we have a need for self-actualization and the desire to serve a greater propose, to belong to the broader community as a valued and respected community member who adds community value. NLP aims to enable the alignment of our ego (ambitions) with our soul (our higher purpose) and integrate this alignment into the broader organizational and cultural system. The NLP strategy of modelling, which is firmly established in cultural theory, is an effective way to develop new behavioural, cognitive, and emotive strategies that will help management teams prosper in a dynamic and often unpredictable environment and work based culture.

References

Anderson, D. and Anderson, L. (2010) *Beyond Change Management*, Pfeiffer.
Bandler, R. and Grinder, J. (1975) *The Structure of Magic, V1*, Science and Behaviour Books.
Dilts, B. R. (2016) *Generative Collaboration*, Dilts Strategy Group.
Dilts, B. R. (1998) *Modelling with NLP*, Meta Publications.
Dilts, B. R. and Delozier, J. (2000) *Encyclopedia of Systematic Neuro-Linguistic Programming and NLP New Coding*, NLP University Press.
Hatfield, E., Bensman, L., Thornton, D.P. and Rapson, L.R. (2014) *New Perspectives on Emotional Contagion: A Review of Classic and Recent Research on Facial Mimicry and Contagion*, Interpersonal.
Maslow, A. H. (1943) A Theory of Motivation, *Psychological Review*, 50: 370–396.

6 NLP and the Law of Requisite Variety

Introduction

This chapter will review the operating philosophy that NLP is built around which could be categorized under the meta-idea '*The Law of Requisite Variety*'. NLP has a conceptual structure around which its capacity for practice as a change methodology is enabled. I call this the '*architecture of ideas*'. I do not think that practicing NLP methods without having a fundamental appreciation of these foundational ideas benefits either the trainer or the practitioner. I invite you to think about these ideas as resources you can use as a conscious change leader to broaden your perceptual map and, thus, increase the range of your behavioural, cognitive, and emotional flexibility.

The Law of Requisite Variety

There is a general principle in NLP that advocates the quest for a 'richer perceptual map' of the world. This involves developing multiple perspectives regarding an object of interest and building a collection of conceptual frames of reference through which we can consider reference objects. Dilts (1998) calls this principle 'The Law of Requisite Variety' which originated from Systems Theory. The law advances the idea that we need to be continually adapting and changing our social strategies to ensure that we maintain and build upon our desired social results. This means that we must always be open to reviewing strategies that have served us well in the past and perhaps in the present and look for opportunities to change or transform these if required. This is the principle of Personal Mastery as developed by Peter Senge (2006) and Organizational Learning as developed by Chris Argyris (1990). Dilts (1998, p. 9) states that the underlying principles governing The Law of Requisite Variety is that "*in order to successfully adapt and survive, a member of a system needs a certain minimum amount of flexibility, and that flexibility has to be proportional to the potential variation or the uncertainty in the rest of the system.*" For Dilts the person with the greatest behavioural, cognitive, and emotional flexibility in the system will be the 'catalytic' force for change. He perceptively notes that this has significant implications for leadership in organizations. In terms of

52 NLP and the Law of Requisite Variety

conscious leadership mediated through NLP applications The Law of Requisite Variety is a meta-guiding principle that motivates the quest for self-mastery over our behavioural, emotional, and cognitive flexibility to maximize our intra and interpersonal skills.

Senge (2006), in his seminal book *The Fifth Discipline*, implicitly advances the principle of The Law of Requisite Variety with a five-point framework he argues is required as a catalyst for the emergence of the learning organization.

The five disciplines are:

1 Personal mastery of our craft
2 Exploring and challenging our mental models of the world
3 Vision building and sharing our vision with others
4 Encouraging team learning through generative collaboration and dialogue
5 Adopting a system thinking perspective towards organizational development and change

The Law of Requisite Variety also applies to the world of change management in organizations. The wider and richer the perceptual map that the manager can develop and access, the deeper the understanding they can glean regarding situations and the wider range of strategies they can conceptualize. For example, if we think of strategy we can think of emergent strategy, planned strategy, localized strategy or even micro, or macro strategy. We may have a concept relating to strategy enabling us to develop concepts such as unconscious strategy work. These are all different conceptualizations of strategy work and they enable us to structure our strategic thinking around multiple perspectives. Compare this to leaders with strategy as a core function who, at best, can only think about strategy as the, or our, strategy in the singular. Clearly their perceptual map is poorer and, thus, their capacity for considering strategic thinking is more challenging, unless, of course, they have a gift for strategic thinking and practice. Imagine, though, the benefits to a naturally gifted strategic thinker if they also had a very rich perceptual map regarding the sociology of strategy work.

NLP provides an operating philosophy which resonates very strongly with The Law of Requisite Variety which is based upon an architecture of ideas, each of which can be flexibility catalysts. I have identified 12 meta-ideas, or flexibility catalysts, that belong to the conceptual structure of NLP and form its guiding paradigm and I will review each of these below.

1 The world as we know it is our own social construction

This idea advocates the belief that the social and natural world does exist independent of mind (Berger and Luckmann, 1966). All we can do is form sense impressions of the social and natural world. These sense impressions are products of active sense making and are based on symbolic systems that are, themselves, social constructions through which humans allocate meaning to objects that they signify as important in their world. This meaning-making process is the basic dynamic of all world cultures. All human beings will identify with a group culture through which they will share meaning systems. Human beings will also have idiosyncratic meaning systems that are relative to themselves on a personal level. Meanings drive emotions which drive attitudes which, in turn, drive our choice of social strategies and our resulting behaviours. This cycle is what NLP practitioners call change work. NLP practitioners assume that everyone has their own world view and that this should always be respected regardless of how strange it may appear, unless, by a global standard, the world view is unethical and harmful to others. Detailed below is a list of the primary sense-making mediums that NLP practitioners study when facilitating change processes in both individuals and in groups.

- **Meta-programmes** can be considered as software programs of the mind. If we use the metaphor that advances the idea that the mind is like a computer then our perceptions – and thus our attitudes towards these perceptions – are simply experiential symbolic programs that we run mentally that filter our experience and drive our behaviours. For example preferring high level details is a meta-programme we call 'chunking up', while a preference for minute details is a meta-programme for 'chunking down'.
- **Belief systems** either enable or limit our growth. An example would involve the belief that underpins the transmission model of change leadership that advances the principle that managers are the planners and bring the intellectual power to a change project.
- **Value systems** either enable or limit our social results and strategies. An example would be either valuing involving stakeholders in generative dialogue during a change project or in contrast valuing top down engagement methods.
- **Modalities**, are the our primary sense-making systems, such as visual, kinesthetic , audible, taste and smell. The term modality is used in NLP circles to refer to these systems.
- **Sub-modalities** are the sensory-based characteristics of our modalities such as sounds, visuals, feelings, smells, and tastes. For example, if we think about a past change project we will naturally focus in upon specific sub-modality characteristics such as the people involved, the locations, the emotions we anchored, the things that were said, how they were said and by whom. Each time we think about the modality experience it will fire our internal awareness of the sub-modality structure.
- **Sensory systems** are our five senses known in NLP circles by the acronym VAKOG (visual, auditory, kinaesthetic, olfactory, and gustatory). Our sensory system acts as a significant filter regarding empirical experience and social construction and they delete, distort, and generalize our experiences.

54 *NLP and the Law of Requisite Variety*

- **Predicates** are the sensory-based words that reveal our lead or preferred sensory system. For example, words like 'see', 'hear', 'feel' are all predicates.
- **Lead sensory system** is the sensory system we prefer to use to make sense of and judge the world as we experience its phenomena, for example, visual, or kinaesthetic.

In terms of flexibility, the NLP strategies of meta-reflection and state management have a range of techniques that help us to calibrate the resourceful nature of the actual content of all the above and induce specific transformations when required. This is a core conscious change leadership skill set and is based upon the principles of critical thinking and reflexivity (Boddy, 2017).

2 We possess the capability to reconstruct our meanings

This idea is rooted in the first presupposition that the world, as we understand it, is a social construction, an interpretation of some external reality that we construct within our minds and which we hold to be real. It advances the premise that human beings are active meaning-makers, that the world as we know it is our invention and that we can author our realities as we deem fit and proper depending on the purpose our social constructions serve. In NLP terms, we can work on our own, and on clients' established meaning systems to change these and, thus, break the cycle of meaning-making and behaviour and recurring emotional states by accessing the following resources:

- Unconscious memories and thoughts
- Modality structures
- Trance induction
- NLP patterns

Our attitudes, emotional states and social behavioural strategies are products of our sense-making and, thus, meaning-making processes. As we build these we can deconstruct and reconstruct established constructs; and, if we chose to, we can make deliberate meaning constructions and, thus, select our attitudes, emotional states and, of course, behavioural social strategies. Therefore, we must take responsibility for our social results.

When we internalize this perspective, we can build in ontological flexibility and be comfortable and, thus, tolerant of the interpretations held by others, even when these appear to contradict our own. Ontological flexibility also ensures that we can adapt our social strategies to evolving shifts in our meaning systems. The opportunity to reframe our reality constructions is made far more accessible to us and these skills enhance our capability as conscious change leaders. This principle also concurs with the work of Alvesson and Sveningsson (2008) who advance the idea of change leaders as 'meaning-makers'.

3 We can be authors of our social identities

In NLP terms, if our identities are products of meaning-making then, again, we choose to accept social identities, or we do not. Others cannot impose an identity upon us; we agree to adopt a social identity or we do not. Identity can be either the most enabling or disabling social device in terms of our social development as human beings. Identities are fluid and dynamic; they are not static. Therefore, we would reject the statement 'I am this kind of person', or 'He is that kind of person'. In contrast we would say 'I choose to be like this kind or person'. Or 'He chooses to be like that sort of person'. This change in language is incredibly important for conscious change leaders as it implies a powerful NLP principle that advances the premise that who we are, who we can be and who we will be are choices that we make. This does not dismiss the deterministic argument of class; for example, we recognize that economic, social, and cultural factors can present significant challenges to our emerging identities though they do not define us. We define ourselves and, thus, once we decide the kind of identity we wish to adopt we can then also identify the resources, for example modelling, to help us enable the establishment and then the wider social recognition of these identities. This flexibility of identity construction is necessary if we are to emerge as capable conscious leaders and coaches to enable such identity work in others.

4 We can change our emotional state at will

Central to our model of conscious change leadership is the ability to calibrate our emotional states and, when required, either pre-programme these in advance of a specific social encounter or meta-reflect on a primary emotional state and change its form if we feel it is proving to lack utility. For example, if we are to deliver an important presentation then the ability to recognize excessive anxiety and shift this to a state of confidence would be an incredibly useful conscious change leadership capability and NLP provides techniques for doing just that.

It is important to understand that our emotions are products of our attitudes which result from our meaning-making processes. Our emotions and attitudes do not, or should not, lead us; rather we should consciously choose them and lead them, they are our resources and, as such, are there to help us be the best version of ourselves as change leaders.

Our attitudes are based on a scale of like to dislike and, thus, we classify the objects of our attitudes on a scale of importance versus unimportance (Maio & Haddock, 2009). Our attitudes are locked into our belief system and, therefore, our expectations of how everything in the world we define as objects of our attitudes should operate. This means that we have both cognitively and culturally wired into our attitude system a programme of predisposed judgements. If, or rather when, our attitude objects do not match with our judgemental models we call forth emotional responses that will be intense

56   *NLP and the Law of Requisite Variety*

depending on the degree of valence we place on the attitude object. The following spectrum of emotional responses in terms of intensity levels will occur when attitude objects do not meet with our prejudged expectations.

Scale of importance of attitude object to the self

1	2	3	4	5	6	7	8	9	10

Emotional intensity elicited

Low	Medium	High

Our emotions are controllable variables that we can influence. When we are faced with incongruence between our expectation of an object of our attitude and its empirical manifestation our emotions do not simply engulf us with a life-force all of their own. We enable the emotional process through our choices. It is well understood in some cultures that crying over bereavement of a loved one is not an acceptable emotional response. Some communities are well-known for holding 'wakes' which are particularly celebratory and festive. Family and friends stay up during the entire night during a wake, and watch over the body of the deceased to honour their life while celebrating. How emotions are experienced, expressed, perceived, and regulated varies as a function of culturally normative behaviour by the surrounding society. In Japanese culture, emotional expressions are tightly circumscribed. This means that emotional expressions are cultural products. Our culture teaches us which emotions are appropriate for cultural situations. However, we forget that our emotions are social resources that we have culturally learned from others. We demonstrate emotional expression unconsciously and unreflectively. If our emotional expression varies from normative expectations, it is regulated by our peers. The conclusion one draws from this scenario is that, through NLP, we can access our unconscious resources and consciously choose, moderate, or intensify our emotional expressions.

5 We can model excellence of capability in others

When Grinder and Bandler initially developed their framework, and understanding of NLP in the mid-1970s they did so with the central aim of developing a modelling technology that is easily taught to others and which enabled the modelling of excellent practice in others and reproducing their results. They analysed the methods of Dr Milton Erickson as a therapist and broke these down into learning units or 'patterns' that they could learn themselves and apply in practical situations with clients and then document these patterns and teach them to others through NLP practitioner courses.

They studied Erickson very closely and mapped out each discreet strategy that he employed as a therapist to build a catalogue of the patterns. This modelling process implies that we can all study what people do and learn how they do it. NLP provides the learning methodologies we need to do the modelling with success.

For example, if someone is a very successful presenter it is not only their natural charisma that works; it may be that they adopt a presentational strategy that paces the world view and the active experience of their audience. They may match their audience's lead representational systems by employing a mix of auditory, visual, and kinaesthetic predicates. They may employ a mix of social strategies that involves the audience at the level of their own identities and they may access the unconscious mind of the audience and utilize their inner resources as part of their presentation. These methods are what NLP modellers call 'patterns' and they can be learned and adopted from people who are excellent at some task or another.

An appreciation of one's capability as a modeller gives the conscious change leader incredible behavioural, cognitive, and emotional flexibility. We simply identify an area for improvement and a role model who demonstrates a high level of competence in this capability and then start to model them.

6 We can design and operationalize our future self

Much of our existence is based in the here and now, in the moment of each day. We operate on a conscious level dealing with mundane or interesting social activities to manoeuvre through the day. We may have ambitions in terms of what we want to be and what we want to experience at a future point in our lives. This process is called ambition. However, much of the time ambitions remain ambiguous or top level social constructions that serve to comfort us through the gritty reality of our day-to-day existence. We can lack definition, emotional substance and a strategic framework of activities that move us towards the realization of our ambitions. NLP can enable us to correct this flaw in ambition management.

Through NLP we can access our unconscious mind and build a future self that possesses all the attributes we desire. We can envisage this future self along our timeline, perhaps a year, two, three or even 10 years in the future. We can dissociate from this vision of our future self and watch what we do and see how successful, fulfilled, and happy we are. We can then associate with our future self directly through an NLP technique known as imprinting and kinaesthetically experiencing what our future self is feeling. Then we can 'anchor' this experience in our unconscious mind and place our future self in a place that we will arrive at and meet that version of our self through the passing of time.

This process of socially constructing a vision of our future self and meeting with it by building the memories we will have in the future, now in the present, and anchoring these will drive us unconsciously towards the end state

58 *NLP and the Law of Requisite Variety*

which is when we meet our future self and realize that they are us and we are them and that we are at one with them and living as them. We have achieved our ambitions.

Having an awareness of this capability and a belief in its enabling properties in terms of identity work is a crucial property of the effective conscious change leader, particularly when one is coaching either formally or informally behavioural, cognitive, or emotional flexibility in others. Being able to co-author with others a developmental road map based on personal identity work connected to vision, mission, purpose, and ambition that they commit to and which guides their choices regarding social strategies is a central conscious change leadership capability. NLP provides a range of techniques that can enable this social construction process.

7 We can regress backwards through time to change meaning systems

NLP practitioners are sensitive to the idea of evolutionary memories. Our unconscious mind reaches operational status whilst we are still in our mother's womb. As soon as we sense our environment we start forming memories. This means that our memory formulation is linear. It has a starting point and an end which we assume is when we die. NLP practitioners employ a useful metaphor through which we can appreciate this concept which is referred to as a 'pearl neckless'. Each pearl represents a modality experience that we have memorized, and which is stored in our neurological vaults as a memory. It is within the structure of our modalities, the sub-modality structure, that our values, beliefs, assumptions, identities, and attitudes are formed. Often if we are experiencing the totalizing impact of a limiting belief that is manifesting with toxic effect on our lives, the best way to treat this is to regress back along the pearl neckless to a point before we had the limiting belief. We can then, through meta-thinking, locate the formation point of the limiting belief and deconstruct its sub-modality structure and then re-construct it but with different sub-modalities and, thus, a different meaning thereby changing our personal history and freeing ourselves from the toxic impact of the limiting belief in question. This can be a very intense and peculiar experience, but it is a very effective NLP methodology.

For example, I once had a traumatic and disturbing association with two colleagues whom I used to regard as personal friends. By employing the pearl neckless metaphor, I could view all the modality pearls that constituted my relationship line with these people. I could enjoy the immense friendship we had shared, the support and loyalty they had given me and the respect we had for one another. These modalities stood before the specific modality that generated a significant source of disappointment and upset. I chose to focus in on the positive modality experiences and, thus, reduced the significance of the one large negative, marking it down to experience. I consequently chose my attitude, selected my emotions, and constructed my own unique perspectives. Again, the ability to choose which element of experience we identify with demonstrates cognitive and social flexibility.

8 We all possess the resources to manage any of our problems

NLP practitioners do not solve the problems that people have, their gift is enabling us to work with our own talents as meaning-makers and to access our own inner resources and solve our own problems. In this way, NLP practitioners are closer to the model of organizational development. Thus, a principle has evolved in NLP circles advocating the idea that we have the resources and capabilities to manage our own problems. In many ways, NLP practitioners are trained coaches who can coach you to be the very best version of you, who coach you to solve your own problems, to model excellence in others and to dispose of limiting beliefs and to realize your ambitions. This principle forms a powerful belief that drives a very optimistic view of human nature in change leaders. If they believe that all people have the inner resources to manage their problems, then they will naturally orientate towards an identity that seeks to collaborate and enable the realization of the potential that lies within all of us. This provides the catalysts for a coaching culture to emerge and a dilution of the traditional paternalistic leadership style.

9 Be curious not judgemental

This principle of NLP is central to understanding rapport-building processes and mastering relationship management through the establishment of active rapport. Human beings have a powerful tendency to orientate their social expectancies around their own model of the world. As individuals, we naturally adopt an ethnocentric perspective which privileges our own standards, values, and assumptions over those of others. When this happens in a group context we experience cultural hegemony or group-think. The ethnocentric character of the individual is predicated on a system of predisposed judgements relative to social phenomenon. An ethnocentric approach to sense-making and cultural inculcation is profoundly useful in that it provides group cohesiveness and social stability as well as functioning as a teaching device. Our culture is built on an ethnocentric character and our schools, colleges and universities award qualifications based on the judging of the knowledge claims and capabilities of students. Managers often judge the performance of others from the basis of their own subjective opinions and from formal performance management criteria. So, it is difficult to avoid an ethnocentric position that is based on a system of concrete judgements.

However, if the ethnocentric character of the group and of the individual is to operate without a counterweight to limit its extreme influences then a state of toxic ethnocentricity can evolve which we call 'cultural hegemony'. This phenomenon is characterized by low tolerance towards alternative perspectives and cultural relativism. Cultural and individual differences are given no

60 *NLP and the Law of Requisite Variety*

discursive space. This means that learning is stunted, and individualism devalued. This situation is the antithesis of NLP.

In NLP circles a counterweight to ethnocentric and judgemental behaviour is encouraged which is to be critically self-aware of one's own world view and to encourage the expression of the world view of others and seek to understand the point of view of others. This perspective of curiosity is one that is characterized by a desire to learn from others, to understand the motivations of others, to gain insight into the meaning behind people's acts and talk. This process of curious behaviour is essential if one is to pace the reality of the other with the aim of distracting them from their reality and leading them towards new meaning constructions and, thus, new reality perspectives. It is an essential strategy to secure rapport with people.

10 Rapport is the key to social success

In their book 'Introducing NLP' O'Connor and Seymour (1990, p. 234) define rapport as: "*The process of establishing and maintaining a relationship of mutual trust and understanding between two or more people.*" Rapport is the aim of NLP. It is the meta-guiding principle of NLP. No NLP pattern can be effective unless one has established rapport with the client. Beyond the practice of NLP, the ability of the individual to function competently and with success in the broader social world is hugely influenced by their ability to establish rapport with people. For change managers rapport-building skills are essential. The ability to build rapport with your peers, your customers, your team members, and your line managers is a source of substantial competitive advantage that can provide you with the edge over others who are competing with you for scarce resources and rewards. Selling, which is arguably the basis of all business success, is dependent upon the sales team or person establishing successful rapport with their customers. Companies which are in the product development business need to have strong internal and external rapport with both suppliers and customers to emerge as a learning organization and produce a learning culture that enables innovative product designs before the completion. In political organizations, such as local authorities, rapport with constituents can, and often does, keep the ruling party in power. In today's media friendly and globally accessible society the ability to maintain positive rapport with pressure groups and wider society stakeholders is a basic competency for the ongoing development and survival of the organization. NLP provides a framework of methodologies which can, on their own and in operation with others, provide you with enhanced rapport-building skills.

11 Uptime and downtime

The bedrock of NLP is the idea that we all have access to conscious and unconscious mind. This concept can be usefully thought of as uptime and downtime. The former involves conscious thought that we are aware of. This is when we can literally hear our own thoughts; we can visualize the objects we are thinking about; we can feel the presence of others. Conscious thought is the main medium through which business academics channel management thinking and sense making. To think at a conscious level is often assumed in mainstream management as rational thinking. It is presumed that to think rationally and intelligently we must be conscious of our thinking. Therefore, the desired state of cognition and sense making is uptime in management circles.

However, within NLP we think that to channel attention mainly towards the conscious mind seriously limits creative thinking and sense-making. NLP practitioners acknowledge, and even privilege, downtime or, as it is conventionally known, the unconscious mind. The unconscious mind is the database and control centre of all of our sense-making functions and memories. From the moment we can think, we form sense impressions and we store memories. These memories do not disappear; in fact, when we form an impression of someone or of a non-human object these impressions form into memories which, literally, become part of us, we never lose them. Much of our sense-making takes place at an unconscious level and this sense-making drives many of our attitudes and social strategies and, thus, generates many of our results. NLP shows us how to access our unconscious mind and work with these resources to become aware of parts conflicts, or limiting beliefs that may be contributing to attitudes and social strategies that are hindering our development. Also, many of our values and beliefs operate at the level of unconscious thought and NLP also shows us how to loosen the lid on our conscious mind to access in a thoughtful and sensitively aware way unconscious thoughts.

The ability to move purposefully between uptime and downtime is characteristic of the 'Mindfulness Movement' that is permeating the corporate world. It is also the foundational capability to enable a successful conscious leadership identity. We cannot manage our internal states, such as our emotions, thinking patterns or beliefs and values, if we are always in uptime. We need to be able to access, at will, downtime states to work with our inner world and bring forth the changes in states that we require to be successful conscious change leaders.

12 COACH versus CRASH state

The final principle that, I think, merits attention is the idea that we must all work towards the attainment of COACH state in our daily lives. COACH state is a 'super resourceful' mind-set that enables high performance conscious leadership. A fundamental aspect of conscious change leadership is being able to self-calibrate one's states and to manage these accordingly. The COACH and CRASH state models provide us with a tool for doing this.

Connected: You experience a high level of connection with stakeholders.
Open: Your mind is opened more fully to new ideas and perspectives.

62 *NLP and the Law of Requisite Variety*

Attentive: You fully experience being attentive to your own needs and the needs of general stakeholders.

Centred: You develop a sense of being fully centred and strong as you become more aware that the roots that give you strength are vividly brought to life.

Holding: You can hold challenging emotions and make them work for you productively.

In contrast to COACH state we have CRASH state which is a super toxic negative state or mind set. CRASH stands for:

Contracted: Feelings of lack of connection with the organization and one's colleagues.

Reactive: Not having time to reflect and being led by one's emotions.

Action paralysis: Continually replaying events over and over in one's mind and building toxic emotions.

Separate: Feeling alone and lacking in trusting relationships within the workplace.

Hurting: Feeling undervalued, underwhelmed, regretting not having the chance to really make a difference at work.

Concluding thoughts

This chapter has reviewed the ideas framework which NLP is built upon. And I have sketched out the 12 key ideas of NLP. Other NLP trainers and practitioners may include other meta-ideas, although these are the ones that impressed me the most. The meta-theme or idea that underpins NLP and provides its source of value to conscious change leadership is The Law of Requisite Variety. Each of the 12 principles I reviewed, if internalized as part of the belief system held by conscious change leaders, are, in themselves, incredibly useful resources as they increase our flexibility and broaden the variety of social strategies we can access as we lead social and cultural change in organizations. The next chapter will complement the ideas framework reviewed above and consider the nature of the core paradigm that NLP orientates around.

References

Alvesson, M. and Sveningsson, S. (2008) *Organizational Culture: Cultural Change Work in Progress*, Routledge.

Argyris, C. (1990) *Overcoming Organizational Defenses, Facilitating Organizational Learning*, Allyn & Bacon.

Berger, P. and Luckmann, T. (1966) *The Social Construction of Reality*, Penguin.

Boddy, D. (2017) *Management: An Introduction*, Pearson.

Dilts, B. R. (1998) *Modelling with NLP*, Meta Publications.

Maio, R. G. and Haddock, G. (2009) *The Psychology of Attitudes and Attitude Change*, Sage.

O'Connor, J. and Seymour, J. (1990) *Introducing NLP Neuro Linguistic Programming*, Mandala.

Senge, M. P. (2006) *The Fifth Discipline: The Art and Practice of The Learning Organization*, Random House.

7   The NLP paradigm

Introduction

NLP is an area of practice and to be competent in this practical concern one should appreciate that NLP is also a social philosophy. It has a cultural paradigm that functions as an expressive engine to produce the beliefs and values that an NLP practitioner should adopt and express. This philosophy is transferable to the world of organizational change and will enable outstanding conscious leadership.

At the centre of every community is the cultural paradigm. This serves as a repository of assumptions, values, preferences and organizing archetypes that govern the expressive options of each community member. The paradigm provides stability and order to the organization through a select grouping of world views, high level abstract beliefs, assumptions and values that are expressed empirically through cultural themes. At the centre of the paradigm are the cultural themes, or the unquestioned assumptions that subsequently give pattern to organizational culture.

As with every learning community within NLP circles there is a cultural paradigm which functions as the expressive engine of the community. It guides and enables the value system and, to a large degree, influences how the field will develop. The early developers of NLP have made these cultural themes explicit through their work, thus revealing the underlying paradigm of NLP. Throughout this chapter I have selected 10 meta presuppositions that are widely recognized as being at the heart of the NLP cultural paradigm for review Whilst not all NLP practitioners will follow this paradigm, most will be familiar with its content. The NLP paradigm provides a set of filters through which change leaders may direct their attention inwardly and outwardly and act towards the world in general.

1 The map is not the territory

This presupposition advocates the principle that we are all map-makers in that we make subjective maps of our experience which we use to guide our interactions with others. However, these maps are not to be taken as objective concrete accounts of a reality that is fixed and proven, rather as creative symbolic representations of experience. We unconsciously delete, generalize, and distort our experiences so that we can function in the world. This fact means that we will all have slightly different or even sharply contrasting maps of the world and it is this symbolic map-making process which drives the development and active reproduction of organizational culture. An important conscious leadership capability is recognizing other people's maps and being curious to understand the positive intentions that lie behind their construction. It is arguably not possible to create a generative field of change practice based upon collaboration and accessing the collective intelligence of the group if we do not recognize, acknowledge, and seek to understand and then integrate multiple maps of reality. Also, once the conscious change leader accepts and even welcomes contrasting maps held by others they become more secure within themselves in that they understand that these other maps are not challenges to their authority, they are simply alternative maps. The basis of dialogue (Dixon, 1996) is built upon tolerating and seeking to understand the maps that stakeholders create and hold and establishing psychological safety in groups so that our maps can be understood and respected and given recognition.

2 There is no failure only feedback

For NLP practitioners, there is no such thing as failure. We reframe failure as an opportunity for constructive feedback so that we can move forward with a richer model of the world to move closer to our goals. Every experience has the seeds of learning embedded in its structural content and we can access this learning if we are open to the idea that it exists. If we take the view or, rather, frame an event as a failure then we effectively close our minds to how we can leverage value from the experience and this framing creates a toxic memory that may inhibit future personal and group development.

When we consider that we have failed at something we define that something for what it is and, in doing so, we build walls in our imaginations that make the quest for realizing our ambitions even harder to achieve. But these walls are not real. They are our own socially imagined constructions. They result from the bricks and mortar of our meaning system and the words that we employ to build these. Change the words we use and we change our perceptions, our belief systems and our attitudes and we may build bridges that link experiences together in common pathways that lead to our ambitions rather than walls which obstruct our journey. For NLP practitioners, there is no such thing as failure. There is only feedback. This semantic strategy is truly transformational. We work towards success. We prepare for success. However, we acknowledge that to be successful in terms of realizing our ambitions we must take full advantage of all learning opportunities that are relevant to the ambition we are chasing. Therefore, any situation that takes us closer to our ambitions is an opportunity for constructive feedback; it is

66 *The NLP paradigm*

neither a signifier of failure nor a setback; it is always a step forward, closer to our goals.

We can learn from every situation and utilize these learnings to our advantage. When we define our state as one of failure we close off the feedback loop and shut down the opportunity for learning and freeze our progress in relation to our goals and related ambitions. For example, I always had an ambition to become a managing director of a major enterprise. I eventually gained an interview for such a post. I did not get the job and it was destined to go to another. I did not fail. I was very successful in that I had now broken through to the interview stage for a highly important social role. I had enjoyed the competitive experience associated with such a role and I had moved my identity closer towards its full realization. These responses are examples of treating the experience as one of feedback and not of failure. This kind of attitude will eventually take you to your desired future self if you apply it diligently.

A critical aspect of change leadership is building a culture of organizational learning. If we as change leaders advocate a culture which identifies situations as failures then we are making the possibility of establishing a learning culture or a learning organization far more problematic. By looking at every situation in-terms of 'feedback' we can maintain an open mind and a curious attitude which permits curious investigation. Instead of blaming and punishing, in a climate characterized by psychological safety we generate curiosity and seek to learn from every situation. We ask ourselves the question "That's interesting, what can I learn from this feedback?" Of course, we will feel emotions such as disappointment, sometimes frustration and even anger though it must be recognized that these are emotions to be held in a resourceful way and if they prevent organizational learning then the potential capital to be gleaned from feedback is lost to us.

3 We own our results

This is a difficult presupposition for many people to internalize. Things happen to us and sometimes they are not particularly enjoyable. They may challenge our socially desired notion of self and threaten identity constructs that we hold dear and are, therefore, protective of. However, things often happen to us because of us. For example, I once worked for a business and was made redundant. I could have resented this event and blamed the senior management for the decision. However, I took responsibility for my own redundancy. I understood the economic and internal political conditions and acknowledged my decision to stay with the firm in the first place and my weak political position in the management team at that time. I owned my own redundancy and this attitude allowed me to progress with optimism and without anger or hatred. Subsequently, I was fully reinstated as the political situation changed and I think my attitude made this reversing decision easier for senior management.

The NLP paradigm   67

For conscious change leaders the capability of accepting responsibility for one's results and avoiding blaming others is a critical attribute. It is very unlikely that people will trust in a potential leader who appears to shirk their responsibilities and seek to place the fault with team members. For example, if a group does not respond effectively and generate successful change outcomes, as unpalatable as this may be for some, it does signify a failure in group leadership. If one can accept this fact, then one can learn from the situation and meta-reflect. The process of meta-reflection opens the door towards transforming the emotional, cognitive and behavioural strategies we have formed as habits and testing alternatives when engaging in what Dilts (2017) calls 'leadership moments' in the future. Meta-reflection involves raising our conscious awareness regarding our cognitive, emotional, or behavioural strategies and treating these as primary states and using the meta-state of curiosity to examine a specific primary state, for example anger, or avoiding confrontation, or the way in which we interact with key stakeholders.

4 We possess the freedom of choice to determine our attitudes

I touched on this theme in the previous chapter though its importance to conscious change leadership cannot be overstated. There is little argument to be made with the claim that the attitudes that stakeholders adopt towards change programmes and their leaders are significant catalysts for both success and failure. An important feature of attitudes is their source of agency. Our attitudes are our own inventions they are not the constructions of others and they are not artificial impositions on the part of others on to us. Often, we beguile ourselves into believing that our attitudes are because of other people but this is a delusional social strategy to adopt. It does have a purpose, though, in that it absolves us of responsibility for the attitude, the emotional state it elicits from us, the way we behave towards an attitude object and the social results we achieve. Viktor Frankl (2004), who survived four years in German concentration camps, wrote of his experiences that:

> Everything can be taken from a man but one thing: the last of the human freedoms – to choose one's attitude in any given set of circumstances, to choose one's own way.

Dr Frankl was right. He understood whilst enduring hell on earth that he had a resource that the Nazis could not deny him, his free agency as a human being to own his attitude. He could have elected to hate the Germans and the Capos who brutalized his community of prisoners and who murdered his family instead, he chose to try to understand them, to build rapport with them so that he could survive. He chose not to hate them post-war as he did not wish to be a prisoner in his own mind and thoughts re-hashing past

68 *The NLP paradigm*

experiences and eliciting emotions of hate and bitterness that would engulf his very existence. He chose an attitude to use his experiences in positive ways to help humanity and to give credit to the memories of his murdered family. This principle is at the very heart of NLP. To be truly free is to have control over your choice of attitudes.

Thus, when we are operating as a conscious change leader and we find ourselves with an attitude towards an aspect of our role that is not resourceful we can welcome this, examine it from a state of curiosity, establish what positive intention it brings to us, understand the reality frame we have created towards a social object that we are applying the attitude towards and then either embrace and own the attitude or change it if we feel it is not proving to be resourceful. A good example is attending progress review meetings with senior stakeholders. We may hold an attitude that 'they' are not supportive encounters and that some members are more interested in identifying flaws than generating support. This attitude may generate a defensive emotional and behavioural state in us. If we meta-reflect and unpack the subjective dynamics behind our reality frame and attitude we can then create a reframe and select a more resourceful attitude. For example, if we take the NLP principle that advances the idea that people always have positive intention behind their behaviours we can reframe the progress meeting as an opportunity to share our work and challenges with our peers. We can embrace their feedback and look to learn from it. We can programme our minds to be thankful that we have a stage to express ourselves and to engage with other committed people who, at a level, are interested in our success. This reframing will stimulate alternative attitudes and emotional, cognitive, and behavioural states that will influence the group states at every level. This, of course, is only possible if we own our attitudes and are open to the process of meta-reflection.

5 People make the best decision at the time with the resources they have available

This principle of NLP when internalized on the part of the change manager will generate a greater capacity for tolerance and understanding. It affords the other a great deal of respect in that it advances the view that, regardless of what they would have done, we make decisions that, at the time, are the best decision they could have made allowing for the resources we had available. For example, once I had an issue with the way a direct report was interpreting their role and enacting it. I made sense of their actions and attitudes through a filter that was my 'model' of the role and how one should enact it. This led to tensions between us and I decided to dissociate myself from the individual concerned, which led to a breakdown in management relations. If I had the resource of meta-mirror which enables first, second and third party perceptual positioning, I would have had greater resources, and if I had known how to access different emotional states to enrich the influence of applying the meta-mirror, I would have made very different decisions which, in all probability, would have generated different relationship outcomes.

6 Respect the world view of others

Sometimes, we assume that all around us see a situation the same way that we do. This is a natural consequence of being an individual. We assume without critical reflection that our reality is a shared reality, that it is an accurate representation of the world around us. This is a significant fault line in understanding that often causes problems when one is trying to lead change work in an organization. It is very likely that our world view is simply that – it is our world view – and the world view of others will most likely be subtly different and can often be radically different. By world view I am referring to the ways in which we frame experience and interpret the meanings of the content and context of these frames of reference. For example, take a management team meeting and a presentation on the part of the CEO on the need for cultural change. Whilst the CEO may feel confident that their world view is readily available and generally shared, it is highly likely that all participants will have contrasting world views regarding the culture at work, what it is and what aspects need attention in change management terms. It is critical that change leaders are sensitive to these differences, can elicit their articulation and, most importantly, respect their differences and are able to pace the experience as expressed by others. A failure to do these things often leads to a breakdown in the collaborative spirit of a change team.

7 People always act with a positive intention

Sometimes we fail to understand the motivations that lie behind the actions people choose to take in response to a given social situation. There is a tendency across Western management culture to adopt a judgemental and critical view towards the actions of others if they do not fit in with our own deeply held world view. If we internalize the NLP principle that people always have a positive intention behind their actions then we can, instead of judging, try to be understanding and curious and to establish what their positive intention is. For example, someone who is openly cynical of a change proposal may be driven by the positive intention that provides them with comfort and protection from change anxiety. By rejecting the change proposal and adopting an openly cynical attitude they dilute the anxiety linked to their insecurity regarding coping with the responsibility of a change leader. If people sense an understanding as opposed to a judgemental state in change managers there is an argument that suggests they will be more open to persuasion, and more open to the provision of the psychological safety provided by their leader that could enable their acceptance of and engagement with the change process.

70 *The NLP paradigm*

8 The meaning of your communication is in the response you get

The number one fault line that dominates the change management literature is the idea that change failure results from poor communication between key stakeholders. It is rarely appreciated that when dealing with communications of feelings and attitudes verbal communication represents less than 20% of the meaning that people create when making sense of someone's communication. Body language and voice tone contribute the other 80%. Also, we actively delete, distort, and generalize meanings from the messages we receive as we filter message content through our beliefs, values, and assumptions. This means that, regardless of the meaning we intend, the meaning we generate is the meaning created on the part of our audience in response to our communication. Therefore, we need to work hard on communication techniques and constantly apply ecology checks to evaluate the degree to which our intended meanings are accepted by our audience.

9 We can shift perceptual position at will

As I discussed earlier, often we are trapped in our own world view and fail to recognize the existence of contrasting world views held by others, some of which we may work alongside every day. This is known in NLP circles as holding the first perceptual position which involves experiencing the world in our own shoes. We can also adopt the second and third perceptual positions. The second perceptual position involves stepping into the shoes of another and fully experiencing their world view and the associated filters and emotions. The third perceptual position involves adopting the identity of an independent observer so that we can observe ourselves interacting with others. This process was developed by Robert Dilts and is known as the meta-mirror. It is an extremely valuable change management strategy as it provides us with a very rich perceptual map through which to plan our decisions and take actions.

10 Resistance is a sign of poor rapport

Building rapport with key stakeholders is a critical part of the leadership process. Building rapport is simply a social skill that we all have the capacity to develop. Rapport can be defined as 'the ability to elicit positive responses from the other'. This ability is an essential competence required to establish you in a leadership role. Rapport builds trust and strengthens relationships which, during periods of intense change, are critical human resources. If people are resisting change management efforts this can often be considered as a sign of poor rapport between potential change leaders and followers.

There is no doubting the quality of a relationship can be defined by the strength of rapport people have with each other. Rapport involves an incremental social process that opens up channels for dialogue both internal and external to one's self. This is an unusual idea; the concept of internal versus external rapport. What this means is that you are both internally congruent in relation to your assumptions, values, and beliefs and externally congruent with others. When you are in a state of internal rapport you are in a high performing state. When you are in this state of mind other people sense this and if you then build rapport with them you have both internal and external rapport and this is a very powerful resource state to be in. Robert Dilts refers to the idea of people avoiding '*airplane mode*' which means that one should not close our channels to the wider field, that is, the collective intelligence of all of us that surrounds each individual and which is, to some degree, accessible but only if our channels are open.

Concluding thoughts

The basic premise of NLP is to study the social construction of experience and to be sensitive to the nature of our internal paradigm which generates our social strategies and, thus, our results. NLP adopts a systems approach that asserts the view that all human beings coexist as part of the wider field and, therefore, the greater our behavioural flexibility, the more adaptable we can be in response to the feedback we are receiving from the field around us. We can only achieve behavioural flexibility if we are able to self-calibrate our own behaviours, identify the attitudes that generate these, work introspectively with the values and assumptions that shape our attitudes and restructure these when necessary. NLP provides the technologies to do this.

NLP offers a philosophy for organizational change leaders through which they can encourage the diffusion model of change leadership. The NLP paradigm can offer change leaders a framework of filters through which they can operate behavioural strategies that are congruent with new-age leadership practices that will resonate with a modern workforce. The NLP paradigm also holds the promise to spread throughout organizations to generate a paradigm of leadership thought that, I think, is better equipped to meet with many of the challenges associated with a rapidly changing global structure of organizations.

References

Dilts, B. R. (2017) *Conscious Leadership and Resilience*, Dilts Strategy Group.
Dixon, N. (1996) *Perspectives on Dialogue*, Center for Creative Leadership.
Frankl, E. V. (2004) *Man's Search for Meaning*, CPI Cox and Wyman.

Part 2
Applied NLP

8 Building the case for change

Introduction

This chapter will address a significant aspect of change leadership which involves building the case for change (McCalman & Potter, 2015). Throughout this chapter I will review NLP analytical models that can support traditional change management tools. The process for building the case for change usually involves analysis of the key change drivers that the organizational leadership has become consciously aware of. This analysis speculates on the influence these change drivers will have upon the organization. The case for change tends to be loosely or tightly built around this analytical process. The major flaw in this process is that it tends to be conducted in isolation by senior managers and can even be what might be described as a desk top exercise. Someone in a strategy position literally sits at their desk and conducts an environmental analysis of change drivers and drafts a change management report for an important stakeholder group. Sometimes, as a tick box exercise they may include some focus groups through which they generate data using traditional MBA strategic planning tools such as SWOT (strengths, weaknesses, opportunities, and threats) analysis, stakeholder mapping, and PESTEL analysis (political, economic, social, technological, environmental, and legal change drivers) (Johnson et al., 2011). This overtly rational approach is the antithesis to generative dialogue and collaborative working. It is a silo approach to strategic planning and change diagnosis which ensures a clear disconnect is maintained between the 'thinkers' and everyone else. This creates a lack of stakeholder engagement and ensures that a rich fault line is created that runs through the cultural and subjective fabric of the change community.

There is nothing wrong with using the strategic tools described above, assuming that you do so in a collaborative way that accesses the collective intelligence of the wider stakeholder group and is based upon interactive strategies, many of which are the topic of this book. However, even if one does this there remains a problem. The problem is the lack of direct association with the actual analysis on the part of key stakeholders. The process is too analytical at a level of dissociation. What is required is a counterweight to the dissociated strategic planning tools; NLP provides such a counterweight which

76 *Building the case for change*

will provide the focus of this chapter. The counterweights are the 'S.O.A.R. model' and the 'S.C.O.R.E. model'.

SOAR model

The SOAR model is an analytical tool that was developed by Artificial Intelligence experts and adapted by Robert Dilts co-founder of NLPU, located within the grounds of The University of California Santa Cruz. SOAR stands for the following.

State: A state is defined as the particular condition that 'someone' or 'something' is in at a specific time. The SOAR model focuses in upon the following in terms of their states: (1) the environment, (2) behaviours, (3) capabilities, (4) beliefs, (5) identity, and (6) mission. The analysis involves determining the past, current, and desired future state of content elements of each of these variables. This process of comparison enables users to build a shared picture and understanding of the content of their changing environment at the level of strategic vision, culture, behaviours, capabilities, and change drivers. The methodology which will be described later in this chapter may incorporate the abstract and dissociated methods of PESTEL, SWOT and stakeholder mapping with associated techniques such as perceptual position-taking across a timeline and multiple neurological levels.

Operator: The operations that we make that result in changes in states. The operators are rooted within our sensory representations of our neurological levels and the sub-modality structure or sensory characteristics of our perceptions and understandings. An example would be directly associating with an experience and describing its form and content, then directly dissociating from the same experience, and perceiving it either from a distance or from the perceptual position of someone else. This operational move would change how we understand the experience, our intensity of emotional attachment resulting from a shift in the sub-modality structure of the original perception. The insertion of the 'A' in the S.O.A.R model simply means 'And' which is used as a link to connect the three main elements together. This presents and opportunity to further develop Robert's model which I think is an interesting idea and in-keeping with the developmental nature of NLP.

The operators are simply the strategies we employ or have employed that have created our past and present results and may well influence or create our future results.

Results: What would a change in state look like? How do we describe and measure success? The SMART model is useful for this stage. In specific terms what would a change in state look like? How do we measure the changes? What activity do we need to undertake? How realistic are our change ambitions? How far down our timeline will the changes take place?

The SOAR model enables NLP practitioners to explore a client's relationship to fundamental aspects of the ecology that underpin the wider social field. The model can be used to build a picture of the changing field that the organization is operating within to guide the development of change management programmes to ensure the organization evolves in a healthy way in relation to the environmental field. The field is the content of the social domains that constitute society at large. The SOAR model enables analysis of operational situations across the wider environmental field from the vantage points of:

- Perceptual position (first, second and third)
- Timeline (past, present, and future)
- Logical levels (environment, behaviour, capabilities, beliefs/values, identity, and mission)

As an analytical change technique, the SOAR model facilitates reflexivity and sense making regarding:

- The change drivers that have been, are currently or will be active in the environment.
- The type of behaviours that have served the organization well in relation to its environment in the past, in the present and potentially in the future.
- The type of behaviours that have not been resourceful to the organization in relation to its environment in the past, the present and, if allowed, in the future.
- The type of capabilities that have served the organization well in relation to its environment in the past, in the present and potentially in the future.
- The type of capabilities that have not been resourceful to the organization in relation to its environment in the past, the present and, if allowed, in the future.
- The type of beliefs that have served the organization well in relation to its environment in the past, in the present and, potentially, in the future.
- The type of beliefs that have not been resourceful to the organization in relation to its environment in the past, the present and, if allowed, in the future.
- The type of values that have served the organization well in relation to its environment in the past, in the present and, potentially, in the future.
- The type of values that have not been resourceful to the organization in relation to its environment in the past, the present and, if allowed, in the future.
- The type of identities that have served the organization well in relation to its environment in the past, in the represent and, potentially, in the future.
- The type of identities that have not been resourceful to the organization in relation to its environment in the past, the present and, if allowed, in the future.
- The sense of mission that has served the organization well in relation to its environment in the past, in the present and, potentially, in the future.
- The sense of mission that has not been resourceful to the organization in relation to its environment in the past, the present and, if allowed, in the future.

78 Building the case for change

This is an exhausting process. It needs to be completed over a few days and involves total immersion in the process. However, when we consider the cost of change failure due to a combination of lack of engagement and weak beliefs in the case for change then this is a very worthwhile time investment. It does also require complete commitment to fully engaging in the process involved.

A blend of NLP methods

The SOAR Model, originally developed by Robert Dilts, incorporates three major NLP techniques including: (1) timeline, (2) perceptual positions, and (3) neurological levels.

Timeline

Timeline is the process through which we catalogue and store all our sensory experiences (Dilts et al., 2010). We have our past, present, and future. We can imagine that we can float above our timeline and view it from an objective position. This is an amazing capability that all human beings possess; in doing so we can move up and down our timeline. We can also build memories today that we will experience in the future and float down our timeline to fully associate in the events that generate the memories we are programming ourselves to experience. Timeline is an excellent strategic and personal development tool. Timeline is a very effective strategic planning tool for management teams and sits very well with techniques such as the neurological levels framework and scenario planning.

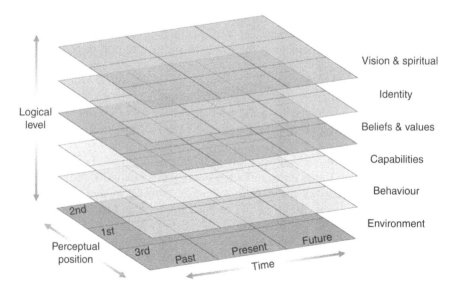

Figure 8.1 SOAR Model

Perceptual positions

Under normal circumstances we tend to predominantly perceive the world from our own subjective perceptual position. In NLP terms, this is called adopting the first perceptual position. When we are in the first position we are directly associating with a social event through our own subjective model. If we rely on our first position to the exclusion of other perceptual positions then this leaves us with a perceptual map that, arguably, is impoverished. To counter this and enrich our perceptual map we can adopt the second or third and fourth perceptual positions through a process of empathetic imagineering. The four perceptual positions are defined below.

First position: This is your own perceptual position as you, yourself, experience it. You are fully associated in the situation and living it as if it is happening right now. An example would be a change leader in the moment experiencing a social situation such as a strategy meeting.

Second position: This is the perceptual position that is the position of an 'other'. It is as if you are in the shoes of the other person and you are walking, seeing, hearing, feeling, thinking, believing, etc., as if you are this person. An example would be the change leader identifying with a colleague and empathizing with their unique model of the strategy meeting from their perspective.

Third position: From third position, you are like an interested, but not directly involved observer of the other two. It is a useful position for gathering information and noticing relationship dynamics going on between them. An example would be the change leader identifying with an objective outsider and empathizing with their unique model of how they see the change leader and their colleague making sense of, expressing and inter-reacting at the meeting.

Fourth position: This is a perceptual position which is a synthesis of all the others, a sense of being the whole system. From this position, you can see the genesis and effects of all the other positions and their interactions, and notice large patterns which transcend individual identities, parts, and relationships.

Switching between these different positions provides us with multiple vantage points from which to perceive a phenomenon of interest and, thus, enrich our map of reality thereby giving us greater sense-making resources. It also enables the development of empathy and greater rapport between conflicting stakeholders. Finally, it increases our behavioural, cognitive, and emotional flexibility and choices.

The Logical Levels Model

The SOAR Model is made up of six conceptual 'floors'. Each floor represents an element of the Dilts Logical Levels Model shown in Figure 8.2.

The logical levels are an analytical tool that was developed by Dilts (2003), although based on the earlier ideas of Gregory Bateson. The principle that

80 Building the case for change

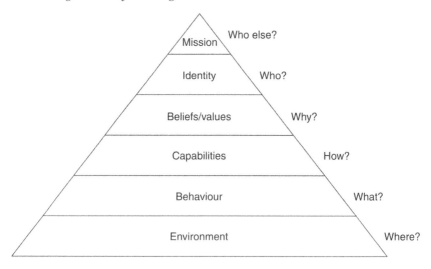

Figure 8.2 Logical Levels

underpins the neurological levels model is that we are all part of a system and a change in one aspect of this system can and will result in a change in the other elements. Let us look at the following example.

> Karen works as Head of Strategy for a major public-sector organization. Traditionally, for over 30 years, the government has 'gifted' the services the organization provides to the public with no requirement to compete for the work through a competitive tendering process. Karen undergoes the SOAR model as part of a strategic change workshop. She considers the environment within which the organization operates. Karen notices that there is a trend of questioning the legitimacy of public sector organizations to deliver services that they have not competed for. This questioning process was being driven by austerity cuts following the financial crisis of 2008, conducted through the media with headlines such as those seen in Figure 8.3.

Stage 1: Karen recognized a fundamental change driver was re-shaping the business environment and that her organization needed to learn how to compete against other service delivery models and prepare for the eventual competition.

Stage 2: It was necessary to consider how this change in the state of the environment would influence behaviours. Historically and in the present most of her senior colleagues behaved as if there was no need to internalize a culture of commercial logic aimed at building defensive strategies based on market forces. These behaviours needed to unfreeze, remodel then refreeze to support the changes in the strategic environment.

Building the case for change 81

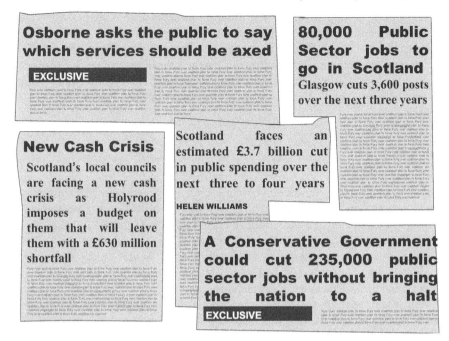

Figure 8.3 Media statement

Stage 3: This stage involved Karen thinking through the past and present capabilities that were directly associated with the state of the environment when lacking competitive drivers. She knew that her colleagues needed to develop marketing capabilities and change management capabilities involving cultural change work if they were to be able to operate competitively and, thus, successfully in the future.

Stage 4: Karen reflected upon the nature of the values and related beliefs that had maintained the behaviours and capabilities of the past rooted in the belief that there was no need to compete for the work and that the government would simply provide this. This change would involve the generation of a new belief system that supported the need for valuing skills such as change leadership and marketing.

Stage 5: Karen also understood that there was now an important strategic question emerging from this analytical process: What kind of organization are we to become? She was concerned about the issue of organizational identity. This suggested thoughts about branding and the ways in which the organization's stakeholders identified with the organization. For example, how did the general staff identify with the organization? Did they see it as a department or as simply their employer? Karen felt that the idea of creating sense making channels with the staff to create a common identity perhaps based upon the idea of the organization as a 'businesses' was now required.

82 *Building the case for change*

Stage 6: This stage involved revisiting the mission of the organization. The mission offered a strategic vehicle for uniting key stakeholders behind the commercial logic and emergent strategy of the organization. The need for developing commercial capabilities and new behaviours integral to a new identity based upon recognition of strategic change drivers in the environment to justify redefining and energizing a common mission, Karen felt, was a strategic priority.

The jungle gym

Dilts and Delozier (2000, p. 698) describe the SOAR model as a jungle gym, a tool through which we can complete a conceptual workout focusing in on past, present, and future states and developing NLP-led interventions to change the nature of the states under examination if required. In their work *Encyclopedia of Systematic Neuro-Linguistic Programming and NLP New Coding* (2000) they present a robust description of the SOAR model and how to apply it as a change process. They recognize and describe no fewer than 45 different analytical frames that a participant could create as they work their way through the jungle gym that is the SOAR model. For example, if we take the **first phase** which involves the first timeline stage of 'past' we can follow each of the five operations involved in creating the frame.

1 First perceptual position associating with a past frame of the environment.
2 First perceptual position associating with a past frame of organizational behaviours.
3 First perceptual position associating with a past frame of organizational capabilities.
4 First perceptual position associating with a past frame of beliefs and associated values.
5 First perceptual position associating with a past frame of the self and organizational identity.

We could include a sixth operation from Dilts' neurological levels model which is mission. The next two phases of completing the jungle gym would involve the participant repeating the above process though concentrating on the present and the future aspects of the organizational timeline. This deeply involved analytical process develops an extremely rich perceptual map of the change issues facing the organization and their dynamics.

Phase 2 concentrates on the second timeline stage of 'present' time and, again, the participant would go through each of the five operations described in Phase 1.

Phase 3 concentrates upon the second timeline stage of 'future' time and, again, the participant would go through each of the five operations described in Phase 1.

The overall result is a composite multidimensional and extremely rich perceptual map of the challenges facing the organization that are deeply meaningful to those who undertook the jungle gym SOAR Model exercises. Whilst this process may not be practical regarding involving all stakeholder groups in totality, it is practical in regard to a representative sample of key stakeholders. It is also a practical model for involving a core representation of senior and middle management to build a powerful sense of a shared case for change and a specific view of what needs to change, why it needs to change and even when it needs to change. The next part of the process would naturally involve designing the content and form of the overarching change technologies, many of which are described in this book to actualize the change process.

Summary of the SOAR model

The SOAR model as an analytical device also enables enhanced understanding of key stakeholders' perceptions and attitudes towards the project. It enables skills audits to be conducted at various stages in the project life cycle. It also facilitates reflective learning and the identification of the skills required going forward down the life cycle of the project. In terms of identity building it is useful in determining the specific role of each team member at each period of the timeline and reflexive thinking. As an analytical device, the SOAR model facilitates reflexivity regarding changes in the operating environment and the type of behaviours, capabilities, beliefs, and values that are required throughout the project life cycle. Finally, it also serves as an enabling device to build a sense of shared mission throughout the wider project team.

The SCORE model

An NLP methodology that can support the application of the SOAR model is the SCORE model developed by Robert Dilts and Todd Epstein in 1987. This model can be used by a management team involving representatives of key stakeholder groups in a collaborative workshop to build a shared picture of significant challenges facing an organization. The acronym SCORE stands for

- **S**ymptom
- **C**ause
- **O**utcome
- **R**esources
- **E**ffect

The process is straightforward. It would involve an audience of 10 to 200. The audience would be brought together to participate in a SCORE

84 *Building the case for change*

conference. The purpose, aims and methodology of the conference would be communicated in advance of the participants coming together. The meta-aim would be to draft a SCORE change diagnostic and action sheet. Trained NLP coaches would facilitate the collaborative process. The process involves the following steps:

- CEO of the organization would set the scene by delivering a summary report detailing the overall performance of the organization.
- NLP Coaches would set up the collaborative process.
- Participants would be allocated into conversational circles of 10.
- Each team would be allocated an NLP coach.
- The NLP coach would work with the team to review each aspect of the SCORE model in relation to a range of organizational variables.
- Each team would engage in dialogue regarding how best to populate each space in the SCORE change diagnostic and action sheet.
- The findings would then be shared across groups for further discussion and contribution.
- The similarities would be noted, outliers marked for further discussion and duplication distilled down to a baseline agreement regarding inter-pretation and proposed actions.
- The trainer would then end for the day and reconvene within seven days to review as a team the composite SCORE change diagnostic and action sheets and agree a mandate for a change programme.

Detailed below is an example of a SCORE change diagnostic and action sheet from a client we worked with. Their actual name has been anonymized.

Closing comments

The purpose of this chapter was to highlight the various ways that NLP can be used as a strategic planning tool. Its deeply collaborative and engaging character helps to dilute the tendency for an ethnocentric approach to strate-gic change diagnosis and planning which plagues change management pro-jects. The SOAR model can either be used in its totality, or its constituent parts, namely perceptual position mapping, strategic time line and logical levels, can be used as independent change management tools. For example, perceptual positioning can be used alongside stakeholder mapping to develop richer perceptual maps regarding the beliefs, values, and attitudes inclusive of expectations that stakeholders may hold that could either conflict with or enable the aims and ambitions of the change programme. The SCORE model can also be used collaboratively to obtain the total system in the room. These analytical applications are excellent tools for the organizational development practitioner to make sense of their dynamic environment and build a compel-ling case for change.

Building the case for change 85

Table 8.1 SCORE model change diagnostic and action sheet excel services

	Customer Service	Sales	Team-working	Margins	Leadership
Symptoms	Complaints	Falling sales	Silo working and aggressive protectionism	Falling margins	Passive leadership
Causes	Poor service	Poor service	Leadership by exception	Falling sales linked to poor service	Historically stable operation leading to complacency
Outcomes	Negative social media	Share value diminishing	Poor collaboration and weak organizational learning	Weak share price	Fragmentation of operational fiefdoms
Resources	Customer Care Training	Review of existing service culture	External OD intervention	Re-design and launch of branding and marketing strategy	Leadership development programme
Effect	Improved customer satisfaction	Establish a change programme	Potential transformation of team-working dynamics	Injection of confidence into the stock market	Transformation of leadership culture

References

Dilts, R. (2003) *From Coach to Awakener*, Meta Publications.
Dilts, R., DeLozier, J. and Dilts, D. (2010) *NLP 11The Next Generation*, Meta Publications.
Dilts, B.R. and Delozier, J. (2000) *Encyclopedia of Systematic Neuro-Linguistic Programming and NLP New Coding*, NLP University Press.
McCalman, J. and Potter, D. (2015) *Leading Cultural Change*, Kogan Page.
Johnson, G., Whittington, R. and Scholes, K. (2011) *Exploring Corporate Strategy. Text and Cases*, 9th edn, Prentice Hall.

9 Building psychological safety

Introduction

This chapter explores an approach through which change leaders may build a culture of psychological safety (Edmondson, 1999) through NLP to enable the development of the diffusion model of change leadership. In established management practice there remains a disproportionate reliance on the transmission model of change leadership fuelling the 'disengagement epidemic'. The ideas that I am advancing regarding what is required to build psychological safety throughout a change management community are not commonplace in the change management literature. Therefore, it was welcomed that Google, through Project Aristotle, positioned psychological safety as an important aspect of change management processes at the forefront of leadership thinking, at least within the boundaries of California, and Silicon Valley. It is also advantageous that scholars such as Alvesson and Sveningsson (2016) have adopted a cultural and social lens through which to study fault lines in change management projects and have identified what happens at a social and cultural level across an organization if psychological safety is not built into the fabric of the operational culture. Building psychological safety is akin to coating a wall with a primer before you paint it with the surface coating. The primer ensures better adhesion of paint to the surface, increases paint durability, and provides additional protection for the material being painted. Psychological safety functions as a sense-making primer which helps the change project attach to the established culture and provide lasting effects and protection from being undermined.

Don't take short cuts

This chapter approaches change leadership from a critical presupposition which asserts the view point that modern managers know how to design change management programmes. They are proficient as technical engineers of change projects. Throughout Europe and the UK there are over 1,700 business schools offering post graduate management training and which emphasize in total, or in part, strategic change leadership and management.

Building psychological safety 87

Also, it is generally accepted that there is an abundance of accessible literature that offers well-constructed frameworks for structuring a change programme. These models are immediately retrievable via search engines on the internet. However, the critical literature overwhelmingly points towards a need for change leaders to build upon their established knowledge and skills regarding the micro social process required to build an atmosphere of psychological safety. This point is not new and as far back as 1969 in the Addison-Wesley series on Organizational Development Warren Bennis wrote about the need for leaders to create climates of psychological safety to enable progressive OD practices. However, regardless of this recognition it appears that there remains a disproportionate reliance on rational planning techniques with less importance given to behavioural science ideas and methods. Yet, clearly, people are curious as there are over 770 million references to change management on the internet as people seek solutions to their change problems. However, perceptions of complexity often lead to shortcuts as managers attempt to reduce the core concepts into manageable agendas. This over-simplification of the diversity of change work appears to generate the following change management framework (Alvesson, 2002).

1 Diagnose the change problem
2 Establish resource requirements
3 Communicate the case for change
4 Build a coalition
5 Develop a change vision
6 Break the change process down into discrete stages
7 Design a pilot
8 Post-pilot, evaluate outcomes
9 Launch the change programme
10 Celebrate group achievements

The challenge in the practical application of the above framework is the Black Box of social interaction. What is really going on between the people involved in the operation of this model of logical change management? What is really happening at the level of micro sense making that either enables the emergence of psychological safety leading to high performing change leaders and teams or disables such outcomes? NLP offers models of interaction that operate at the micro level of sense making and which address gaps in competency frameworks that enable high performing change teams and leaders. Our model, which enables the building of psychological safety, shows at a very practical level just how a change leader may approach their role with the aim of creating a climate of psychological safety in their operational domains.

It appears that there is an imbedded presupposition in many management communities that advances the idea that managers only have to apply these prescriptions and successful change will occur. The problem with this view,

88 *Building psychological safety*

according to Alvesson and Sveningsson (2016), is that rational and linear models imply a simplicity that does not exist. The sequential model does provide a framework to guide change management efforts; however, if the change manager has no underlying model of understanding and working with social sense-making processes and interactions then the likelihood is mediocre success or relative failure (Collins, 1998).

The conclusion arrived at is that the main problem facing those who are involved in leading change work is a lack of relevant language and ideas rooted in social interaction processes that are specific to change projects.

Mindset and state management

The first stage and central element of our approach is mindset and state management. This is the process through which the change leader develops self-reflexivity and conscious leadership skills. The former involves building competence by reflecting upon one's emotional, behavioural, and cognitive strategies and questioning the resourceful nature of these in terms of goal achievement and intra- and inter-relationships. The latter involves the development of competencies which enable the change leader to select the emotional, cognitive, or behavioural state they deem to be the most resourceful. These competencies are the core enablers of effective soft skills development in change leaders.

Caretaking

The second stage of our approach starts with the most basic yet fundamental aspects of a change project which is caretaking. This stage involves the change leaders taking care to build fundamental environmental conditions that are supportive towards change participants' psychological condition. This stage involves managing the psychogeography of the venues that meetings are to take place, managing one's own internal states and enabling the emergence of highly resourceful emotional states in others. This stage has the meta-objective of change leaders being able to elicit COACH state in their teams when approaching and experiencing social interactions. The name we give to this process is 'building a coaching container' which is an aspect of leadership and relationship management that is often overlooked. Part of the role as a care taker is to generate a coaching container within which people can feel confident in their relationship with you to express themselves without fear of any attack on their sense of self. This involves building a relationship through which we, as the 'lead influencers', act as 'caretakers' of the environment that our audience is to operate within during their interactions with us. This involves accepting our responsibility to 'calibrate', 'pace', 'elicit' and 'lead' the others into a state of psychological safety within which they feel no threat to their established identities. This involves providing a safe and supportive environment.

Rapport building

The third approach, building rapport between the change leader and their teams, provides the social glue which holds a climate of psychological safety together. To build rapport with an individual, or with groups one can either operate instinctively, cross one's fingers and see what happens, or one can model the rapport-building processes of highly successful change leaders and internalize these social strategies to a level of unconscious competence.

Detailed, in Figure 9.1 is the NLP Model of Rapport Building which involves multiple interactive strategies, the sum of which enables generative rapport between stakeholders. I will review this model in detail in the chapter on rapport building. I will argue that establishing a state of rapport between stakeholders is a critical leadership process and that, in the absence of rapport, effective and authentic change leadership may not be possible.

Framing experience

The fourth stage involves change leaders operating as meaning makers. This active identity involves the daily framing of experience in ways that generate collaborative social construction through dialogue between the change leader

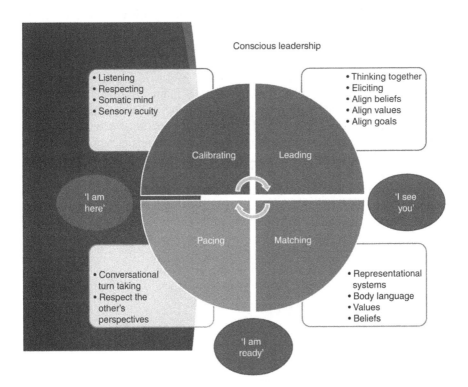

Figure 9.1 Model of rapport building

90 Building psychological safety

and their stakeholders. Put simply if the reality frames constructed by the stakeholders are very different from those of the change leader a state of onto-logical incompatibility will develop which will create social distance between the members of change teams and disable the potential for collaborative working at an authentic level. The change leader needs to be able to pace the world view of different stakeholders and hold the challenging feelings that will be stirred because of ontological incompatibility. They need to aim towards a state of ontological congruence which involves holding two frames simulta-neously; the one that you are initially committed to, and another that is in the making.

The meta-objective during this stage of our model is to avoid stakeholders conflicting over reality frames and being open to reviewing the merits of their frames based on empirical evidence and through dialogue, constructing a common frame of reference that the team can all agree upon which serves as a basis of collaborative action.

A final aspect of building psychological safety that can be enabled through NLP applications is the sensitive art of giving feedback.

Giving fish and stretch

In NLP language we refer to feedback as 'providing fish and stretch' (Dilts, 2003). The idea of giving fish provides us with a way to re-programme our attitudes towards providing feedback. The idea is to see the positives in some-one's work or behaviours and to acknowledge these. For example, if someone prepares a document or a presentation and shows it to a colleague and the colleague provides no feedback other than to point out spelling errors or aesthetic opinions this is an example of someone imbedded in a critically judgemental model of the world. This does not encourage a relationship of psychological safety between the people involved and impairs rapport building. This is not to say that errors should be ignored, rather that if this is the only feedback offered it is unquestionably unbalanced in the extreme. Thus, it is good practice to learn how to give fish; to detect aspects of a performance or a task achieved that the other person is emotionally and egotistically invested in and acknowledge these with positive affirmations linked to their identity. Only then can we expect the other person to be open to the judgement of the other. This state of openness can only occur if both parties are in a state of rapport. Once we have rapport then we can gently provide stretch to another person. This involves coaching them to build their social, emotional, and cognitive capabilities.

Giving fish

Giving fish is a metaphor for rewarding, recognizing, and encouraging excellent behaviour, attitudes, and performance. The principle behind this strategy in terms of engagement building is that human beings have a psychological need

Building psychological safety   91

for recognition and positive feedback. In the absence of this, the social glue that connects team leaders with their teams and vice versa is very weak. Giving fish is more than a functional task, it is a state of mind, an operating philosophy towards leadership and human nature and a key element of the psychological contract that cements open, trusting, and resourceful relationships.

Importantly, psychologists have come to realize that the psychological contract and its relative the state of psychological safety are only possible if rapport is built between people. It takes time to do this. Yet, in a second, one can break rapport and thus break or fracture the climate of psychological safety one has carefully built up in a project team over time. The fish that the change leader presents to their team must be genuine, from the heart, and the recipient must feel that this is, in fact, the case. Simply performing excessive compliments is a superficial activity that lacks authenticity and will not stimulate rapport; in fact, it can do the very opposite and break or prevent rapport.

Giving fish involves recognizing and emphasizing an aspect of a team member or member's performance in a detailed way that acknowledges best practice. Now let us look at the opposite of giving fish which is giving stretch.

Giving stretch

Giving stretch is a social strategy that is only possible if psychological safety is in place between team leaders and their team members mediated through rapport-building processes. Giving stretch involves inviting another person to accept and consider advice based upon observations concerning the performance or capability of the other person with the aim of stretching their abilities. This is a very difficult activity to perform without clashing with the inter-subjective model of the other. Everyone has their internal model of what good practice looks, feels, and sounds like. These internal models are deeply personal, and we guard them from criticism with emotional force. Often, we connect these models with how we behave or perform and, thus, self-validate our own performances. This means that, inevitably, when someone is giving another stretch they are comparing an aspect of the other person's capability against their own internal model of best practice. This has another thorny element in that to give stretch one assumes that one's model is the correct model and that you, as the provider of the stretch, practice what you preach. As we all know, sadly in management circles, this is not always the case.

These sensitive issues make the practice of giving stretch more challenging. It should be clear that you cannot simply jump in to a new relationship and start freely offering stretch. This will certainly ensure that you do not build rapport and will disable well intentioned leadership activities. The problem is that, often, experienced managers can do just this, unreflectively and habitually. It may be the case that the secondary gain they obtain from this practice is the self-validation of their own perceived worth as management experts in

92 *Building psychological safety*

their area of practice and maintaining a perception of personal control on the work and identities and subjectivities of others. This is a toxic psychology that NLP aims to dilute and reverse.

To give stretch competently one needs to be perceived by the team members as a role model of some kind or another. They need to understand and appreciate the skills and experiences you have that give you credibility to offer fish and stretch. This identity as a role model needs to be earned. These challenging variables evidence just why the time required to build rapport is so critical to achieving successful and productive project team member dynamics.

Style is important

An important aspect of giving fish and stretch is our choice of words, voice tone, body language, and emotional state. These resources need to be thoughtfully selected. As one can appreciate we need to be skilled at matching to build the initial rapport required to open the channels in others to be receptive to accepting our fish and stretch as authentic, sincere, and well intentioned.

The end game behind rapport building in our NLP model is the generation of leadership. Once rapport is in place then if you are to lead, i.e., invite others to accept your fish and stretch then you must be able to elicit a state of mind that is open to your leadership. If rapport is in place, and if psychological safety has been established then you can experiment with giving fish and stretch. If the team members accept your contributions without aggravation and remain open and connected and perhaps even act upon your feedback, then this is evidence that you may have established a leadership/follower relationship within the change project team.

In the exercise that follows we provide examples of how to give fish. Let us say you were attending a team presentation on a change project and feedback was invited. The approach that is aligned with the principles of giving fish would involve the careful framing of feedback statements which start with language patterns such as:

"What I observed in your performance was…"
"What I really liked about it was…"
"What you did that I really appreciated was…"
"The reason that I really appreciated it was because…"
"For me what was particularly impressive about your performance was…"
"The reason for this was…"

The above language patterns are examples of fish.

The above reinforces capabilities that are strengths. This is an essential aspect of leadership; however, we do also sometimes have to 'stretch' the capabilities of our team and we do so using the following language patterns:

"What I observed that could be further developed was..."
"The reason for this is..."
"I really liked when you... and if you were to... I think it could be even more effective."
"The reason for this is..."
"When you... what I noticed was... and if you... I think you would..."
"The reason for this is..."

These language patterns should always be used in total sincerity and when done this way are powerful at building positive engagement and, thus, rapport with team members and encourage a state of learning by being open to the feedback.

Concluding thoughts

This chapter has described an approach that can create an atmosphere of psychological safety in an organization and support the change leadership strategy of diffusion as opposed to the now largely redundant model of transmission. As Google has demonstrated (Duhigg, 2016), if change leaders cannot build an atmosphere of psychological safety then they cannot effectively lead a change programme with integrity. Finally, I briefly reviewed the NLP approach to giving constructive feedback to both re-enforce existing strengths and to stretch certain aspects of our capabilities as change leaders. The next chapter will review the NLP applications one can use to manage stage one of our model Mindset and State Management.

References

Alvesson, M. (2002) *Understanding Organizational Culture*, Sage.
Alvesson, M. and Sveningsson, S. (2016) *Managerial Lives: Leadership and Identity in an Imperfect World*, Cambridge University Press.
Bennis, W. (1969) *Organizational Development*, Addison-Wesley.
Collins, D. (1998) *Organizational Change: Sociological Perspectives*, Routledge.
Dilts, B. R. (2003) *From Coach to Awakener*, Meta Publications.
Duhigg, C. (2016) What Google Learned from its Quest to Build the Perfect Team. *New York Times Magazine*, 25th February.
Edmondson, A. (1999) Psychological Safety and Learning Behaviour in Work Teams. *Administrative Science Quarterly*, 44(2), 350–383.

10 Un-packing the mindset mix

Introduction

In this chapter I will define the concept of a mindset. In doing so I will unpack the mix of variables that generate our mindsets. Our mindset shifts throughout the day. In NLP terms, we would call our mindset a nominalization; the conversion of a verb into a noun. There is a tendency to reframe the process of mind that influences our choices of emotional states, cognitive states; and behavioural states from a process of symbolic interpretation and social construction into a thing, a part of us that is somehow fixed and outside our control. In this chapter I will define mindset as a process, as a verb, that is very much under our control and open to our influence if we can access a meta-reflective state.

If as change leaders we are to master what Dean and Linda Anderson (2010) describe as conscious leadership which calls for an ability of change leaders to access their mindset and adjust their cognitive, emotional, and behavioural strategies and critically review the values, beliefs and attitudes that are state generative, then we must have a model to reflect upon. This chapter will build such a model starting with the central component 'meta-reflection'.

Meta-reflection

When we are experiencing the enactment of the emotions, cognitions and behaviours stimulated by our meaning system we are experiencing a primary state. A primary state is the state of being we happen to be associated with in the moment; for example, the emotional primary states of being happy, or sad, or the cognitive primary states of being curious or bored, or the behavioural primary states of being energetic, or passive. When we are in a primary state we tend not to notice its characteristics or give it a name. Neither do we notice how these states are influencing the energy field we are generating and how this is then influencing the quality of rapport we are having internally and externally. This also means that we are not noticing how our primary states are influencing our social results.

When we access a meta-state, and engage in meta-reflection we are going above the primary state. A meta-state is a state of interest about a state. For example, if I like the idea of NLP then I can develop an interest in NLP. My meta-state is that I like NLP and my primary state is that I have an interest in learning about NLP. My meta-state is above my primary state. It drives my movement towards and into my primary state. My meta-state is a reference point to my primary state. Another example is when we experience a state of frustration, and instead of simply experiencing frustration unreflectively we become actively aware of our state of frustration.

This process we call meta-reflection. It is a critical change leadership skill that is largely underdeveloped throughout the global change leadership community.

Many change leaders are led by their states. They are not consciously aware of this leading process. They enter a primary state, and this influences their choice of social strategy and, thus, their social results. We aim to disrupt this habit. It is our aim to encourage change leaders to lead their states consciously rather than have their states lead them. Conscious leadership involves the calibration of our internal states and intervening in the process via state management enabled by meta-reflection and selecting the primary state that is most resourceful for us in each situation.

Defining mindsets

Our mindset can be defined as a state of mind that results from the combined influence of our selected attitudes, meta-programmes, reality frames, beliefs, values, and emotional states manifesting in our body language. The psychologist Carol Dweck made popular the concept of mindset when she developed the model of a 'growth' and a 'fixed' mindset. Dweck, (2012, p. 6) defines a fixed mindset as: *"believing that your qualities are fixed in stone"*. In contrast she defines a growth mindset as: *"a belief system that your basic qualities are things that you can cultivate through your efforts"*. She argues convincingly that the mindset that you internalize as a habit will significantly influence your social results. Our mindset is the established set of attitudes held by someone. This is an accumulative result of our meta-programs, attitudes, beliefs, and values that generate our social strategies and, therefore, our results. Our mindset is not fixed. It is very plastic and, therefore, we can change its content and structure if we can access *'Meta-states'*.

For example, we may find ourselves adopting a fixed mindset towards learning something new via a planned course of study; alternatively, we may adopt a growth mindset. What is important is that this is a choice we deliberately make, even if this choice is made at an unconscious level of thought. Through meta-reflecting we can audit our mindset and, if we choose to do so, change it. The following table highlights the mindset mix or internal variables that underpin the manifestation of each of the two mindsets, fixed or growth. I have used the example of a study course to flesh out the key points.

The process of mind that we go through to build our mindset involves relations between all the above internal variables. It is not a linear process, it is a deeply complex fusing together of the mindset mix dependent upon the importance of each variable that the unconscious mind allocates that establishes the final mindset.

Our mindsets are incredibly important regarding change leadership outcomes, yet, sadly, the practice of meta-reflecting towards our mindset is,

96   Un-packing the mindset mix

Table 10.1 Mindset mix analysis

Internal variable	Fixed mindset	Growth mindset
Belief	'I don't need this learning'	'I could benefit from this learning'
Value	'I value "doing" not "studying"'	'I value both learning by "doing" and by "studying"'
Emotion	Guarded and tense	Relaxed, attentive, and optimistic
Meta-programme	Away from	Towards
Modality frame directive	'What's the point?'	'This learning is needed'
Attitude	Dislike learning new things	Enjoy learning new things
Somatic anchor	Contracted body language	Open body language

again, not a standard change leadership practice. Hitherto, research studies by organizations such as IBM, the British Computing Society and Google reveal that the inability to reflect upon and shift mindset purposefully is a major fault line undermining change leadership efforts.

Modality Frame Directive

The Modality Frame Directive is our model of the world analysed in micro detail. What this means is that it is a very small slice of our sense-making experience that is framed and used to generalize experience. Some scholars call this phenomenon our sense impressions, schemas, our interpretive frames, or our cognitive maps. Modality frame directives are basically memories or sense experiences we have had in our lives. They are very important as they have meanings attached that we unconsciously assume to be fixed and these meanings drive our attitudes towards things and thus our emotional states and social strategies. Modality frame directives heavily influence our social results. For example, if our early life experience involved our parents tutoring us and believing in us and if our subsequent experience of school is positive then these modalities guide our attitude towards our ability to learn.

Modality frame directives have a structural composition. They have sensory characteristics such as: colour, sound, smell, taste, time, location, purpose, characters. These aspects of the modality frame structure are known as '*sub modalities*'. For example, we may attend a progress meeting with our senior manager to discuss how the change project is progressing set against pre-planned performance indicators. As we experience the meeting in the actual moment we are unconsciously building our modality frame directive. Just as an artist creates their own unique impression of reality, so we create our own unique modality frames. These modality frames constitute our memory of the meeting.

The relevance of this idea for the change leader is based upon the principle that underpins symbolic interactionism as described by Blumer (1969). His first core principle of meaning states that *"humans act toward people and things based upon the meanings that they have given to those people or things"* (Blumer, 1969, p. 2). Symbolic interactionism holds the principle of meaning as central to human behaviour. What is particularly interesting in NLP terms is that these meanings are social constructions that the change leader has, themselves, created. They are not reflections of an objective reality, rather they are maps of a perceived reality, and imperfect maps loaded with deletions, distortions, and generalizations. A central aspect of NLP is that we can meta-reflect upon our modality structures and frames and disassociate from the established content and review and reframe this resulting in a change in the meaning attributed and therefore a change in our attitudes, emotions, cognitions, and behaviours. This is a significant conscious leadership skill.

Somatic anchor

An anchor is any symbol that one associates with an experience. The symbol can be abstract or it can be a material object that you can touch, or it may be a sound you can hear. We also have somatic anchors. These are anchors that we imbed into our physical demeanour. The somatic anchor is the posture we adopt when we think about the modality frame directive. It is an expression of our cognitive and emotional states. It tends to manifest as a closed and contracted physical expression. The somatic anchor not only represents the mindset, it also reinforces it by anchoring it to our psychology. If we regularly enter a particular state it is highly probable that we will fire a somatic anchor. To fire the somatic anchor means to activate the state by physically expressing the form of the somatic anchor. For example, when one sits back sharp and tightly folds one's arms this could be a somatic anchor that puts one into an aggressive or frustrated state. Sometimes we can change our social dynamics simply by reflecting upon our somatic anchors and deleting these from our expressions if they are proving to fire un resourceful states.

It is commonly understood that 'emotion follows motion' and this principle is very useful for us to remember that often somatic anchors become habits. We express the somatic anchor and fire its emotional references unconsciously. For example, entering closed body language posture when attending a meeting one is not connected to reinforces our fixed mindset and enables a decent into CRASH state. Meta-reflection helps us identify these un-resourceful habits and change them.

Anchoring

In contrast to a somatic anchor are visual anchors. An example of a visual anchor that is used for marketing purposes is the McDonalds logo. As the brand logo of this fast food business it is intended to anchor the association of McDonalds in the mind of a consumer with a satisfying and enjoyable catering experience.

98 *Un-packing the mindset mix*

Anything that is meaningful to the self can function as an anchor. Whenever one thinks about an anchor, either at a conscious or unconscious level we trigger an emotional state which generates an attitude and a social strategy. In terms of change leadership, the change leader can function as an anchor in the mindset of change participants and the very voicing of the change leader's name will generate the associated emotional state and behavioural strategies. This has significant implications for change management leadership. An anchor in NLP terms can be understood as any symbol that an individual or group associates with an experience and related emotional states and attitudes.

By simply thinking about the anchor one can access the emotional state that one previously associated with the anchor.

Dilts and Delozier (2000, p. 29) define anchoring as "*the process of associating an internal response with some environmental or mental trigger, so that the response may be quickly, and sometimes covertly, re-accessed*". For example, if some individual wishes to deliver a public presentation with confidence whilst controlling their anxiety levels, they could access a memory of when they had this social and emotional state and think strongly and with acuity about the anchor associated with this experience. The anchor can be any kind of concrete or abstract symbol we choose. By simply focusing in on the anchor we fire the previous experience and use this process to enter the social domain of presenting and bring with us the highly resourceful state elicited. Anchoring is the process through which we accept an experience and store it in our memory for future retrieval.

The anchoring process, when it occurs organically, is arbitrary. However, change leaders trained in NLP can purposefully set up an anchor in the mind of a change audience. For example, they can use change mantras repeatedly to anchor ideas and belief systems to experiential reference points. A change mantra is a short sentence that contains anchors relating to an outcome. Examples of change mantras would be:

- "We are all in this together."
- "If we don't change our jobs are at risk."
- "We are stronger together."
- "We must be competitive to retain and win customers."
- "It is the quality of your work that will determine job security."
- "Together we can build our shared Circle of Success."
- "Our vision is a winning team."

The choice of words is evocative and intended to stir internal representations in an audience's mind and trigger specific emotional states connected with experiential referents. The organization can then design marketing images around these verbal mantras that visualize the empirical context.

Understanding how to calibrate our anchors is a fundamental meta-reflective skill. If our anchors can fire our primary states and if these have such a powerful influence upon our choice of social strategies and our corresponding results, then knowing how to meta-reflect towards our choice of anchors and what they anchor is a fundamental change leadership skill. Also, we must always bear in mind that our audience will have their own anchors. For example, there may have been a past change project that promised much yet delivered little. The language of change leadership may therefore itself be a significant anchor that when fired releases cynical and negative states in your audience connected to past failures. This is particularly relevant when these people may have engaged with optimism and hope in the earlier initiative only to be let down in some way by those in charge of the change project or able to influence its delivery outcomes.

A belief

A belief is simply what we hold to be true about the attitude object that is driving the construction and maintenance of the modality frame directive. Beliefs are reality perspectives we hold to be true about ourselves, others, and the content of the universe. Beliefs can be based on material constructs and conceptual constructs. Beliefs are extremely powerful filters which guide our sensory acuity as we experience our external and internal representations. Beliefs are often unconscious and so, much of the time, we do not think about them. However, they can guide our conscious mind and have a substantial influence on our social strategies of choice and, therefore, our results. For example, if one has a belief that leaders should be strong, decisive, and confrontational then one could spend one's life unconsciously judging people in leadership roles against the model that the belief generates. Our ability to meta-reflect on the nature of our belief system and how the discrete beliefs influence our social results is an important aspect of change leadership.

A good example of this was developed by the management guru, Douglas McGregor, in his seminal work *The Human Side of Enterprise* (1960). McGregor provided an analysis of two contrasting belief systems that managers may relate to. He called these 'theory Y' and 'theory X'. McGregor firmly believed that managers, influenced by their life history, internalize the beliefs associated with either theory Y or theory X. These belief systems heavily influence the kind of corporate and organizational culture that will develop through time. They become the unconscious guiding compass for managers and they are taught through attitudes and behaviours to other managers. Table 10.2 details the model.

It appears clear to me that theory X and Y are both examples of a fixed and a growth mindset. If one is trying to encourage the emergence of a learning culture, then perhaps our choice of mindset really does matter in acutely strategic terms. The challenge for change leaders is whether they are willing to meta-reflect on their belief system and, if required, intervene, and delete beliefs that are proving to be incongruent with the values of the change project and best practice change leadership and replace these with new beliefs that are congruent.

100 *Un-packing the mindset mix*

Table 10.2 Theory X versus theory Y

Theory X belief system	Theory Y belief system
Staff need to be supervised and controlled.	Staff can create self-managed teams.
Human beings dislike work.	Human beings enjoy collaborative working.
Human beings are predominantly financially motivated.	Human beings have a hierarchy of needs and motivations.
Staff need to be explicitly directed.	Staff organize their own work.
Managers need to plan work.	Staff can co-design work-schedules with managers
Staff will avoid responsibility.	Staff seek responsibility.
Staff at work are not creative towards work.	Staff have a highly creative potential if enabled.

A value

A value is the sense of worth that we assign to an attitude object. This is the mechanism that guides our attention and generates our internal motivations. Our value system is directly connected to and rooted within our belief systems and thus our choice of mindset. Values are concepts that reflect the beliefs of an individual or culture. A set of values may be placed into the notion of a value system. Values are considered subjective and vary across people and cultures. Types of values include ethical/moral values, doctrinal/ideological (political, religious) values, social values, and aesthetic values. For NLP a practitioner's values are cultural productions and the batteries behind our social strategies.

Integrity in the application of a value refers to its continuity; persons have integrity if they apply their values appropriately regardless of arguments or negative reinforcement from others. Our values are key drivers of our sensory acuity; they heavily influence what we pay attention to and for how long and to what depth. This is important for change leadership. One would think that it would be common sense to engage in meta-reflection regarding one's own value framework if one is entering a change leadership role. To identify values that perhaps are incongruent with the change project and develop a management strategy for these would be useful. For example, if I am the change leader yet I do not value detail though I value high level description, then clearly this could be a problem. Therefore, if I can meta-reflect on this as I sense my discomfort when someone engages in a detailed account of a change situation, ask myself why I am feeling uncomfortable, identify my lack of value for detail and make a conscious effort to change this and accommodate or even welcome detailed accounts as well as high level accounts then, arguably, I will be more effective and enjoy higher levels of rapport.

An attitude

One of the substantial targets for NLP interventions is attitude. An important premise of NLP is that we can select an attitude and, so we do not adopt an attitude because people make us; we select an attitude as an act of personal power. Therefore, we have the power to change our attitude at will and, thus, change our emotional state and associated behaviour and physiology.

An attitude is defined by Maio and Haddock (2009, p. 10) as: *"an association in memory between an attitude object and an evaluation of it. An attitude is defined as an overall evaluation of an object that is based on cognitive, affective, and behavioural information."* Attitudes drive our reality constructions and they determine our state of mind. Attitudes control our very existence and one could also claim that they have significant control over our destinies. If we are to engage in the artful practice of NLP intervention, then an understanding of the dynamics of attitudes is crucial. Attitudes also vary in valence and strength. The object of an attitude can either be abstract or concrete in form. NLP interventions aim to dilute or strengthen the valence or strength of attitudes.

Attitudes are deeply imbedded in the unconscious mind. The nature of an attitude can be inferred from our behaviour and therefore the NLP technique of calibration is so important. It is what people do, or say, which reveals their attitudes and the nature of these in terms of valence and strength and how attitudes manifest in behavioural strategies. To understand the process of attitude at work one should break it down into its sequential parts.

The cycle depicted in Figure 10.1 illustrates the wheel of repetitive behaviour we find ourselves trapped in that, over time, can have disastrous results for us. NLP is ideally suited to intervene in the pattern and change its structural content by altering the meaning we attribute to the attitude object. This results in an altered emotional state which induces us to select a new behavioural strategy which then results in a new kind of social feedback.

Figure 10.1 Wheel of repetitive behaviour

102 *Un-packing the mindset mix*

An example of this cycle at work would be a change leader who has a phobia regarding public speaking. The act of public speaking is the attitude object and the attitude could be described as a feeling of lacking in confidence that the person has and, thus, a deep dislike of the object. The meaning attribution could be that the person feels that no one is really interested in what they have to say and that they will lose their belief in their material as soon as they start to present their subject. The emotional state thus elicited may be one of intense fear and anxiety. The behavioural strategy adopted may be to simply avoid at all costs the attitude object. The resulting social feedback would be a public perception that the person lacks self-confidence and does not like engaging with people. This social feedback then reinforces the attitude and the object of the attitude. If the person must experience the attitude object then the resulting anxiety and nerves, most probably, will show in their presentation and the social feedback, it is likely, will prove to be negative. NLP aims to intervene at the meaning attribution stage. If one can work with a client to shift the meaning from negative to positive, one can alter the cycle in totality.

Emotion

Dilts and Delozier (2000: 355) drawing from Grolier's Encyclopedia define emotions as follows: "*Emotions are biopsychological reactions of an individual to important events in his or her life.*" Emotions are 'feelings' that we get that cause physical changes in us. Emotions have an important purpose in that they move us to action. If we feel fear we normally flee, or we may attack. These strategies are driven by the intensity of the emotional charge and are influenced by our culture. Emotions initially generate changes in our inner state and then are observable in our physiological state. We can become prisoners of our emotional states. They can become deeply habitulised and ingrained on our physical, cognitive, and behavioural habitus. NLP provides tools that enable one to audit one's emotions and assess their resourceful nature and identify the habits of thought and the modality frame directives that generate the emotional states. Daniel Goleman (1996) has written extensively about 'emotional intelligence' and he advances the idea that we have two minds; our cognitive mind and our emotional mind. Often, the former influences the latter, intellect follows emotional sense making. This occurs at a deeply unconscious level of thought and the sense making of the emotional mind is incredibly quick and outruns that of the cognitive mind. This a basic survival mechanism as in the past our ancestors had to act swiftly based on instinct that triggered defensive emotions if they were to survive. NLP is a valuable resource to enable the development of our emotional intelligence which involves us being able to heighten our powers of empathy, social awareness, internal management of our emotional states and the ability to generate at will emotional states that are highly resourceful for us situations. Finally, emotions generate an energy field around us that can be contagious to others and in some cases can be unsettling. NLP helps us be self-aware regards our energy fields and enables us to change these or increase or reduce their emotional intensity.

Meta-programmes

A basic component of mindset structure is our meta-programmes. One of the fundamental innovations of NLP was the identification of meta-programmes. Hall & Bodenhamer (2009, p.30) define meta-programmes as *"Different frames of mind that colour the way we see and experience the world. Meta-programmes are the mental and perceptual filters for paying attention to information. These perceptual filters govern our attention as our frames of mind or thinking patterns."* Thus, meta-programmes are a fundamental aspect of our mindset of choice, change the meta-programmes we use, and we can either reinforce our mindset or change it quite significantly. Meta-programmes are patterns of thought that guide our perceptual awareness and heavily influence the way we distort, delete, and generalize our experiences. Meta-programmes are biased compasses of the mind that lead us to behave in very specific ways. Meta-programmes navigate our perceptual awareness and provoke selective representation of reality and generate the 'model' for every social strategy we operate. Thus, meta-programmes have a very significant impact on our social results. I shall examine meta-programmes in greater detail in the next chapter.

Closing comments

Most managers will understand software systems such as Excel, PowerPoint, and the Internet. They will have a working knowledge of the processes that support the organization of work. They will no doubt have a deep understanding of the technical aspects of their specific occupational identity, e.g., HR Manager, IT Manager, Services Manager, Production Manager, or Marketing Manager. However, when they enter a change leadership role this knowledge is useful though not enough. They need a working knowledge of how people tick. They need to be able to figure people out and, importantly, they need to be able to figure themselves out. This knowledge is concerned with unpacking the vital mix of variables that influence the form and content of our mindsets. They require a competent understanding of the constituent elements that shape mindset and how to think about this and act towards it. This chapter has presented a model that enables such a learning outcome.

References

Anderson, D. and Anderson, L. (2010) *Beyond Change Management*, Pfeiffer.

Blumer, H. (1969) *Symbolic Interactionism*, University of California Press.

Dilts, B. R. and Delozier, J. (2000) *Encyclopedia of Systematic Neuro-Linguistic Programming and NLP New Coding*, NLP University Press.

Dweck, S. C. (2012) *Mindset: How You Can Fulfil your Potential*, Robinson.

Goleman, D. (1996) *Emotional Intelligence*, Bloomsbury.

Hall, M. and Bodenhamer, D. (2009) *Figuring People Out, Reading People Using Meta Programs*, NSP Neuro Semantic Publications.

Maio, R. G. and Haddock, G. (2009) *The Psychology of Attitudes and Attitude Change*, Sage.

McGregor, D. (1960) *The Human Side of Enterprise*, McGraw-Hill.

11 Meta-programmes

Introduction

This chapter will address the ways in which the mindsets of change leaders can be shaped and changed through adjustments to the meta-programmes we habitually use (O'Connor & Seymour, 1984). The meta-programme we choose influences the nature of the emotional, cognitive, or behavioural state we adopt as a social strategy and these internal strategic decisions have a powerful influence on our social results as change leaders. I will employ the NLP model of meta-programme auditing which will help change leaders to recognize un-resourceful meta-programmes and transform these into resourceful states that enable successful change leadership outcomes. I will also examine a technique known as 'perceptual positioning' as a method of calibrating and changing our meta-programmes through a role-modelling exercise.

Kinds of meta-programmes

Meta-programmes operate at a level of unconscious thought. It is quite possible for a person to go through their life unaware of the existence of their own meta-programmes and the ways in which they influence their social results and, thus, their experience of life in general. NLP enables us to become aware of our meta-programmes, to calibrate them effectively and to intervene in their structural content to change them. If this methodology alone was the only contribution of NLP to the world it would be a significant contribution to serve humanity productively.

Table 11.1 provides examples of 10 fundamental meta-programmes that change leaders should become aware of.

Meta-programmes can be described as filters that select experiential data and we use this data to formulate a social strategy. Our meta-programmes, as biased compasses of the mind, can lead us into COACH state, or they can lead us into CRASH state. The aim of NLP is to develop cognitive flexibility in change leaders so that they can calibrate the meta-programme that is guiding them and, if necessary, change it to a different directional compass if it is not proving to be resourceful and is leading the change leader into

Table 11.1 Meta-programme examples

Meta-programme	Perceptual bias	Relevance to change leadership
Away from or towards risk	Does the change leader gravitate towards risk or away from risk? Do they prefer to remain in their comfort zone or experience situations that stretch them and thus run the risk of damaging their reputation or sense of self?	Change management by necessity involves 'loosening the lid' on the models that people hold as archetypes of 'how' things are and 'how' things work. Therefore, an ability to be comfortable with risk and to even enjoy being out of one's comfort zone is a positive resource for a change leader to have.
Internal or external validator	Does the change leader assess the quality of their workmanship internally and thus 'self-validate' or do they prefer to obtain validation from outside sources, i.e., are they dependent on the appraisals of others?	Change management is a very subjective affair that involves collaboration. The workmanship of the change leader is defined by the quality of their leadership relationships and the change management outcomes. Therefore, the methods through which we define 'well-formed outcomes' is critical to the change leadership process. The change leader needs to be able to seek the views of others to create the performance indicators that define what success will look like. They need external validation.
Match or mismatch	Does the change leader mainly look for differences in relation to the perceptions of others and their own? Alternatively, does the change leader look for similarities between their perceptions and those of others?	Initially when developing a change programme, we are seeking to locate differences in approaches that can be adopted by the organization. This involves mismatching As the programme develops complex problems will emerge that require different points of view and perspectives to be integrated in the change dialogue. This again needs mis-matching. However, there are critical times when we need to match the thinking patterns of key stakeholders to build consensus for change and to cement new ways of thinking and behaving.
Failure or feedback	Does the change leader respond to set backs as 'failures'? Alternatively, does the change leader respond to setbacks as opportunities for 'feedback'?	The issue with perceiving setbacks as 'failures' is that it is both a judgemental strategy and it closes down critical reflection. Perceiving a setback as a feedback opportunity encourages dialogue and organizational learning.
Static or dynamic	Does the change leader view social situations as 'fixed' models of reality? Alternatively, does the change leader view social situations as 'dynamic' and fluid models of reality?	If one considers cultural change, or behavioural change, then one needs a mindset that sees the organization as a fluid dynamic system that is open to change. If one perceives the organization as a closed system that is static and relatively fixed ('that's just how things are') then it would be difficult to imagine a change leader being effective with this mindset.

Meta-programme	Perceptual bias	Relevance to change leadership
In-time or through-time	Does the change leader prefer to experience time as it unfolds (in-time)? Alternatively, does the change leader prefer to 'stand over' time (through-time), to view it as a historical, present, and future construct that is part of a systematic whole?	In-time change leaders may find themselves absorbed by immediate local issues. This can block their ability to 'see' the patterns unfolding because of their actions. Through-time change leaders can take a high-level vantage point and 'see' the timeline that has led to the present and construct a view of how it may unfold going into the future.
Chunking up or chunking down	Does the change leader prefer the 'big picture' which involves 'chunking up' to the top-level details? Alternatively, does the change leader prefer 'chunking down' to the gritty details?	If the change leader prefers chunking up as a dominant meta-programme they may miss the granular details that are shaping future circumstances. The 'Devil is in the detail' as they say. If the change leader prefers chunking down, then they may find themselves stuck in the 'mud' and unable to articulate the bigger picture.
Judgemental or curious	Does the change leader adopt a 'judgemental' approach to others? Alternatively, does the change leader adopt a curious mindset towards others, i.e., they seek to understand their behaviour and the point of view driving it and why they hold it?	A critical competence in a change leader is the ability to understand people and to relate to them. If the meta-programme drives the change leader towards judging people against their own internal models, then this will act as a barrier to building empathy and understanding with others. A state of curiosity is a resourceful mindset for change leaders to be able to access.
Problem or opportunity	Does the change leader perceive challenging situations as 'problems' that need to be solved? Alternatively, does the change leader perceive challenging situations as 'opportunities' to learn, grow and develop?	There is much debate in the literature regarding the idea of 'the learning organization'. The foundation to the learning organization is the capacity of change leaders to establish an organization-wide COACH state. If the mindset is to 'solve' the problem and move on, then arguably this leads to an emphasis on 'closure'. Alternatively, if the mindset is to exploit the opportunity for group learning then arguably the problem gets solved and the organization 'learns' how to learn.
Compliant or strong-willed	Is the orientation of the change leader to comply with the authority of others? Alternatively, is the orientation of the change leader one which resists authority and seeks to demonstrate strong will power?	A significant challenge facing organizations is in-fact a lack of 'leadership'. I adopt the view that leadership involves seeking out differences, encouraging dialogue, confronting challenges, and pushing boundaries. If the change leader has internalized a meta-programme which privileges compliance over independent mind, then perhaps they will be limited in their change leadership capabilities.

CRASH state. This process of reflective thought is called meta-reflection and represents thinking about thinking. As previously discussed, meta-reflection is a process of mind through which we stand over and above conscious thought to review the ways in which our thought patterns (meta-programmes) are constructed and the influence they are having upon us at the behaviour and attitudinal level and thus the influence they have on our social results.

The model meta-programme is extremely useful as a diagnostic tool to gauge the state of an organizational culture across multiple dimensions. Its utility lies in the fact that it starts with the individual as a meta-programme profiling device. Then, by aggregating the number of profiles we can identify meta-programme patterns in a cultural domain and generalize with a high level of confidence about the characteristics of the cultural paradigm of the organization. We can also identify the 'desired' changes that individuals are seeking in their culture and identify group patterns through the aggregation of data collected. Inserted into each of the dimensions, of the meta-programme audit checklist, as shown in Table 11.2 below, are '*meta-programme symptoms*'. Please rank (on a scale of 1 through to 10) each symptom in order of how each variable matches with both your present and preferred thinking style.

It's not a case of 'this' or 'that'

The important observation to make regarding meta-programmes and their relevance for change leaders is that it is not really the case that one type is correct all the time. I am encouraging a contingency approach towards our choice of meta-programmes. The point is to become aware that we have meta-programmes, identify them and understand their content and the direction they point us towards and the ways in which they influence our choices of social strategies and, thus, our results. The key to this process of managing our meta-programmes is critical self-awareness. This process is helped by adopting a different perceptual position which involves stepping into the shoes of someone who uses a different meta-programme to ourselves and building a sense of how it feels to try it on for size, to get a sense of how it feels and the emotions it creates, the strategies the person selects and the social results the person obtains.

The technique developed by Robert Dilts called 'Perceptual Positions' is based upon adopting various perceptual positions to enable for example conflict resolutions. The technique involves imprinting one's self into any one of four alternative perceptual positions.

- First position: one's own perception of a situation or object
- Second position: that of other stakeholders involved in your dynamic
- Third position: that of the objective observer detached from your dynamic
- Fourth position: that of all three positions synthesized to give you a wider perceptual map

Table 11.2 Meta-programme audit checklist

Dimension 1: Organizational learning: fixed or growth mindset meta-programme

	Meta-programme symptom	*Present*	*Preferred*
1	I look forward to participating in a group learning situation.		
2	I don't see the need for formal learning, I prefer learning on the job.		
3	Academic learning regards leadership is not for me.		
4	I value the chance to learn from different sources.		

Dimension 2: State of hierarchy: internal or external validation meta-programme

	Meta-programme symptom	*Present*	*Preferred*
1	I often feel a need to consult my line manager regarding my work.		
2	I rarely feel the need to consult my line manager regarding my work.		
3	I think regular update meetings with my line manager are important for good relations.		
4	I don't really see the benefit in regular update meetings with my line manager for me personally.		

Dimension 3: Leadership ideology: transactional or transformational meta-programme

	Meta-programme symptom	*Present*	*Preferred*
1	I like it when my line manager gets actively involved in my personal development.		
2	If I know what's expected of me and I tick the right boxes for my line manager I am content.		
3	I know if I get the job done I get no hassle from above.		
4	I value the chance to have introspective conversations about the values and mission of the organization with my line manager.		

Dimension 4: Market orientation: necessity or possibility meta-programme

	Meta-programme symptom	*Present*	*Preferred*
1	Marketing is not important in the scale of things.		
2	I would like to get more involved in the marketing process.		
3	Marketing is extremely important and worthwhile.		
4	Marketing is something that we are expected to do.		

Dimension 5: Environmental orientation: inwards or outwards meta-programme

	Meta-programme symptom	*Present*	*Preferred*
1	I enjoy the chance to benchmark what I do against other organizations.		
2	I think that my work is fairly standardized across industry so benchmarking probably would not be that useful.		

3	I value external benchmarking across industries using models such as EFQM.		
4	I don't think there is much I can learn from other organizations in my sector.		

Dimension 6: People orientation: team or production meta-programme

	Meta-programme symptom	*Present*	*Preferred*
1	I like working as a team member on different projects.		
2	I prefer leading my own team to participating in collaborative team-based projects.		
3	I look forward to collaborative projects working across the organization.		
4	I prefer working to my own agenda at my own pace.		

Dimension 7: Strategic orientation: present or future meta-programme

	Meta-programme symptom	*Present*	*Preferred*
1	I am far more concerned with the needs of today than what's required in five years' time.		
2	I really enjoy dealing with operational issues on a day to day basis.		
3	I really enjoy thinking about how we can get better at what we do in 12 to 18 months' time.		
4	If I had to choose between spending a day on what's happening right now or working on a strategy planning session I would take the former.		

Dimension 8: Technical orientation: hard or soft skills meta-programme

	Meta-programme symptom	*Present*	*Preferred*
1	I really value technical skills over soft skills.		
2	I often think about how I can develop my soft skills.		
3	I would promote a person based on their technical skills.		
4	I would privilege soft skills over technical skills.		

Dimension 9 : Service orientation : quantitative or qualitative meta-programme

	Meta-programme symptom	*Present*	*Preferred*
1	When measuring success, I prefer numerical performance indicators.		
2	I value proactively researching customer experiences using open questions.		
3	If sales and profit are in line with budget I assume service standards are effective.		
4	I involve customers in product development projects.		

Dimension 10: Conflict orientation: towards or away from meta-programme

	Meta-programme symptom	*Present*	*Preferred*
1	A critical leadership trait is confronting poor performance.		

2	Inter team conflict is unfortunate yet normal. I don't get involved.		
3	I avoid confrontation whenever I can.		
4	My job is to maintain standards even if it means upsetting people.		

Dimension 11 : Communication orientation : monologue or dialogue meta-programme

	Meta-programme Symptom	*Present*	*Preferred*
1	I try to join meetings with lots of conversation.		
2	I try to encourage conversations between team members when hosting meeting.		
3	I prefer presenting information and inviting questions.		
4	I enjoy short, sharp meetings based on team updates over deep conversations.		

Dimension 12: Reward orientation: extrinsic or intrinsic meta-programme

	Meta-programme symptom	*Present*	*Preferred*
1	My reward for doing my job is economic.		
2	My reward for doing my job is knowing that what I do matters.		
3	My reward for doing my job is security of employment.		
4	My reward for doing my job is the chance to grow and to develop.		

Dimension 13: Social agenda orientation: dreamer or realist meta-programme

	Meta-programme symptom	*Present*	*Preferred*
1	It's important that I do work that makes a difference in the community.		
2	I like the idea of doing work that benefits the community, but we must attend to the needs of the business first.		
3	We don't do enough work for the community.		
4	We could do a lot more work for the community, but we simply don't have time or resources.		

Dimension 14: Management orientation: participative or controlling meta-programme

	Meta-programme symptom	*Present*	*Preferred*
1	I like getting involved in my team's work and providing guidance.		
2	My job is to check what my team are doing and intervene when required.		
3	I enjoy solving the problems for the team and advising them of the best approach.		
4	I always get the team together and we work through our problems together.		

Dimension 15: Team orientation: tribal or community meta-programme

	Meta-programme symptom	Present	Preferred
1	I always defend my team.		
2	I enjoy working across the organization in a collaborative team.		
3	My team has its own very distinctive way of doing things compared with other teams in the organization.		
4	It is important that I get the chance to project manage task forces made up of different team members.		

Dimension 16: Risk orientation: towards or away from meta-programme

	Meta-programme symptom	Present	Preferred
1	Any significant decision must be risk assessed.		
2	If we don't take risks, we cannot grow and develop.		
3	Risk taking must only be done if necessary.		
4	I know if I take a risk and it fails I will not be punished.		

Dimension 17: Change: dynamic or static meta-programme

	Meta-programme symptom	Present	Preferred
1	My main role is to make sure that stability is maintained in my part of the organization.		
2	I think the organization is always changing and my job is to influence these changes.		
3	We need stability if the organization is to be effective.		
4	Dynamic change presents lots of opportunities for growth and development.		

Dimension 18: Conformity: matching or mismatching meta-programme

	Meta-programme symptom	Present	Preferred
1	It is important for me to be seen to fit in all the time.		
2	If I think that people are missing the point it is important that I speak up.		
3	I always encourage people to be honest and express their views even if they challenge my own.		
4	To get on with people it is important that I don't say or do things they may disagree with.		

Dimension 19: Expectancy orientation: optimist or pessimist meta-programme

	Meta-programme symptom	Present	Preferred
1	I always think that change programmes may go wrong.		
2	Whenever I get involved in a change project I look for opportunities to be part of its successful delivery.		
3	I think change programmes should be carefully evaluated in terms of risk before we commit to them as failure is very costly.		

112 Meta-programmes

| 4 | I don't think failure is a good way to think about things, I prefer the idea of treating all outcomes as a form of feedback, an opportunity to learn. | | |

Dimension 20: Detail orientation: chunking up or down meta-programme

	Meta-programme symptom	Present	Preferred
1	It is important to me to understand the detail.		
2	I find detail rather boring and prefer top level information.		
3	When I brief my team, I aim to give them as much information as I can, so they really understand the issues.		
4	I like team briefing notes that summarize the main issues as I think that's all people need.		

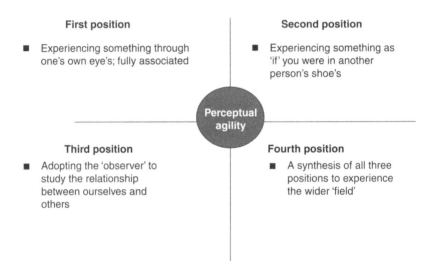

Figure 11.1 Perceptual Position mapping

This model provides us with multiple vantage points from which to perceive a phenomenon of interest and, thus, enrich our map of reality thereby giving us greater sense-making resources. It also enables the development of empathy and greater rapport between conflicting stakeholders. It can also be used as an exercise to identify with role models or as a device to develop one's critical self-reflection skills, and it can be used to understand the perspectives of key stakeholders during change. For example, if I habitually used 'chunking up' (which means being interested in broad brush details) as opposed to 'chunking down' (emphasizing micro details) as a meta-programme I could use the following NLP pattern.

Meta-programmes 113

1 Identify someone who preferred chunking down.
2 I could initially fully associate with chunking up in the first perceptual position and ask myself the following questions:

- What do I believe to be true about chunking up as a strategy?
- Why do I value chunking up over chunking down?
- How do I use the strategy of chunking up?
- When do I use the strategy of chunking up?
- What success do I achieve through chunking up?
- What capabilities do I have which enable successful chunking up?

3 I could adopt the second perceptual position (my role model) and step into their shoes to simulate their thinking patterns, perspectives, emotions, strategizing and appraise their social results. The kind of questions that I would ask myself are:

- What does this person believe to be true about chunking down as a strategy?
- Why does this person value chunking down over chunking up?
- How does this person use the strategy of chunking down?
- When does this person use the strategy of chunking down?
- What success does this person achieve through chunking down?
- What capabilities does this person have which enable successful chunking down?

4 Then I can step out of the second perceptual position and move to what we call in NLP our third perceptual position which is the independent observer who can observe both ourselves and the role model operating their respective meta-programmes and thus get a sense of how others relate to the two approaches.
5 Then we step into the fourth perceptual position which is our reflective learning space, or our meta-position. From the meta-position we can reflect on all three perspectives and this provides us with a much richer perceptual map and awareness of meta-programmes.
6 The next step involves anchoring both meta-programmes, i.e., chunking up and chunking down against the perceptual mapping experience. Then when we need to we can fire the anchors and access either chunking up or chunking down, or even merge the two meta-programmes together to create a middle ground approach to thinking about change management details.

Conclusion

In conclusion, you will enable far more effective change leadership abilities as you start to unpack the meta-programmes that can both block and enable successful organizational transformation. You can intervene in your subjective

114 *Meta-programmes*

processes and restructure your meta-programmes to generate new emotions, cognitions, behaviours, and social strategies. This shift in our own mindset requires meta-thinking and critical self-awareness. It also requires a desire to change and improve upon our cognitive, emotional, and behavioural flexibility. This involves accepting the idea that mind and body are part of one integrated whole.

Reference

O'Connor, J. and Seymour, J. (1984) *Training with NLP*, Thornson.

12 Framing of experience

Introduction

As a change leader, I adopt a social construction perspective. This means that I understand that both the social and the empirical world are not accessible to me in a real and concrete sense. In NLP circles, we all implicitly adhere to this philosophy which is imbedded in one of our more famous presuppositions; *'the map is not the territory'* (Bandler & Grinder, 1975). We build interpretive maps of reality using symbols and their interrelated meanings to construct our maps. Our maps are also products of a filtering process. This filtering process involves us deleting, distorting, and generalizing our experience through our beliefs, values, and representational systems. Therefore, our maps are always just our maps; also, as we constructed our maps, we can deconstruct these and then reconstruct them if we choose to do so.

The contrast to social construction is positivism. A positivist philosophy assumes that we can access reality, that our maps are representations that reflect reality. This means that often change leaders who are in the positivist position completely believe that their perspective or model of the world is the correct one. If others compliment their models of the world then they quickly build rapport, however if they do not then rapport is less likely. This problem plagues change projects and often leads to conflict either covertly or overtly. If our maps are challenged by others this can generate real anxiety as our subjective competence as a leader is interpreted as being under attack. How we choose to react to this will determine the kind of relationships we experience with stakeholders and the quality of psychological safety that can or will emerge in the change teams.

This chapter will explore NLP methods for generating ontological flexibility, which basically means the ability to hold multiple models of the world simultaneously, to respect and pace the models held by others and to facilitate a reframing process through which a shared model can be built by the change teams through dialogue that presents a basis for collaboration and action.

Sense-making fault lines

As previously discussed Mats Alvesson has studied change projects acutely over the last 20 years and, along with Stefan Sveningsson of the University of

116 *Framing of experience*

Lund in Sweden, identifies a myriad of micro fault lines that collectively weaken the foundations of a change programme to the point of collapse (Alvesson & Sveningsson, 2015). What is interesting in their study is that they focus in on the intersubjective nature of sense-making mediated through belief and value systems that influence general attitudes and thus behavioural strategies towards change agendas. They have developed the idea of toxic symbolism to explain the way in which apparently pedestrian actions can be interpreted and socially constructed and transmitted as mini narratives that, taken together as a whole of their parts, frame the nature and credibility of the change programme, its developers, and sponsors in the eyes of the broader change community. This framing process often happens at two levels: at a conscious level mediated through conversations both internal and external to the self, and secondly at an unconscious level of thought. Thus, for change leaders to be successful they need to operate at two levels:

1   The world of strategic planning for change
2   The world of subjective experience and micro sense making

Presented below is an example of multiple stakeholder frames regarding the prospect of strategic change taken from a company that operates Soft Facility Services in the USA.

Karen is the Head of Strategy for Excel Services which provides catering, building cleaning, landscaping and reception services to the world. Karen believes that the 'green' agenda is no longer a fringe issue. She believes that at both an unconscious and conscious level consumers are starting to become more sensitive to environmental issues such as:

- Animal welfare
- CO_2 reduction
- Organic farming
- Fair trade
- Recycling
- Pollution
- Provenance
- Craft development
- Fresh produce

She develops a reality frame that advocates the view that her employer should adopt a 'Go Green' strategy and an international quality framework to guide a transformation programme within their catering divisions. Karen believes that not to do this will result in the operation lagging seriously behind competitors and the operation being framed as lacking legitimacy to trade in the eyes of consumers. Basically, consumers will be ashamed to be associated with the service as it currently stands if this is permitted to be maintained for any serious length of time.

The Head of Purchasing frames Karen's model of the world as a strategic threat to economic stability and is concerned that the cost implications are too great.

The Divisional Head of the catering operation frames Karen's model of the world as excessively impractical and not a strategic necessity. Sales are constant; the operation is efficient and the team very settled. She does not wish to disrupt these conditions and frames Karen as seeking influence over her operations.

The area operations team value stability and predictability and believe that their operations are models of operational efficiency. They frame Karen's model of the world as a criticism of their competencies and decide to challenge her ideas.

The Executive Chef has a parts conflict. He appreciates and is excited by the prospect of fresh food, enhanced craft skills and the chance to explore new supply routes whilst also wanting to 'fit in' with his managers and being concerned about the effort required to change the culture of his kitchen brigades. He is also concerned whether the purchasing arrangements will be adapted and cost also is a major worry.

Analysis

As we can see there are at least five alternative models of the world that are competitors to each other. We can further analyse this and assume that each of the actors holds certain beliefs and associated values that generate their world view and create their reality frame specific to Karen's case for change. This, of course, includes Karen. If we accept the NLP presupposition that everyone comes from a positive place then we can also conclude that the root of this integrity is their belief system. Their beliefs can be assumed at this stage; although, through qualitative research adopting semi structured interview methods and incorporating the NLP techniques called meta-model questions we can accurately determine the beliefs and values a person holds and deconstruct their internal paradigm or meta-world view. This is often what happens in a NLP coaching session with an executive manager. However, at a level of assumption, we can assume that detailed in Table 12.1 are the values and beliefs held by each stakeholder in the case study example.

The challenge for the change leader

Traditionally the advocates of strategic change have relied on their legitimate authority to push through their ideas for change. This is what Alvesson and Sveningsson (2015) refer to as the 'Transmission Model' of change leadership;

118　*Framing of experience*

Table 12.1 Stakeholder values and beliefs framework

Stakeholder	Belief	Value
Karen	Future-thinking and strategic change is required	Continuous development
	Market drives strategic change	Time out to scan and make sense of external change drivers
Head of purchasing	The immediate economic system drives strategic thinking	Lowest cost suppliers
	Their role is to establish stable supply chains	Maintaining the status quo
Head of operations	The business does not need to change its operational strategies	Their 'right' to manage
	The operation works efficiently and effectively	The maintenance of order and creation of predictable conditions
Area managers	Day-to-day operations are what really matter	Stability and predictability and order
	Their job is to check that others do their job effectively daily	Control and monitoring processes
Head chef	Craft development working with fresh produce is a good thing to do	Continuous development of craft and product
	Fitting in with the wider operational team is important for cohesive working	Harmony and stability

top down transmission of authority to lead. What seems to happen, often, is that general stakeholders do not authentically collaborate. Rather, they appear to agree to agree and at a surface level engage with the strategic change agenda. However, there is a substantial difference between image and substance. If the emphasis is on image rather than substance then the degree of collaboration may be very thin. Both practitioner and academic research point towards mindset and culture as significant change blockers in these instances. However, mindset and culture are processes; the problem is that change leaders often nominalize these processes which convert what are verbs into nouns. They assume in doing so that mindset and culture are fixed entities rather than fluid processes which are social constructions rooted in sense-making that are open to change 'if' the change leaders know how to create psychological safety in change teams. Change leaders are required to be

Framing of experience 119

sensitive to nominalizations and reverse these back to their authentic states as verbs. If we view social constructions as processes that we author, rather than as 'things' that control us, then we can greatly enhance our agency to influence the social world as change leaders. This process naturally involves the NLP methodology of content and context reframing which involves changing the meanings we attach to content and context of a given situation to elicit a change in our emotional, cognitive and behavioural states.

The change leader also needs to be able to access their powers of empathy to break free from their own world view and frame of reality and access the frames of others and to understand the beliefs and values that are feeding and supporting their sense-making frames. The technique of perceptual positioning can facilitate such a process.

The change leader would either identify an external coach to guide them through the perceptual positioning process or, alternatively, they can create an '*internal coach*' which involves accessing their unconscious mind and establishing a relationship with a self-identity part of one's unconscious mind and granting it the authority to act as an internal coach. This may seem a rather odd notion. However, if one stops to think about it when we experience internal conflict related to, let us say a decision we must make, we do engage in internal dialogue with multiple parts. For example, going to the gym. One part of our unconscious mind might be reluctant to go and even question if it is worth the effort; it may suggest to us that we can postpone the gym in that moment and catch up another day. Another part might say that we should go to the gym and that going in the moment will be good for us. This is an example of a parts conflict and our inner voice, or inner chatter is the expression of the independent nature of the apparently conflicting parts. What I am suggesting is that we can create an internal part that we can refer to as our internal coach so that we can leverage our capacity for generating internal dialogue to create a resource to self-manage internally referenced NLP techniques such as perceptual position mapping. The pattern is described below.

1 Identify a challenging work-based social dynamic involving a key stakeholder. This could be a reality frame that conflicts with your own. For example, you are attending a meeting to develop strategic choices and you see leadership development as a strategic priority and the other stakeholder feels that it as a luxury cost to be avoided.
2 Adopt the first position and associate into the dynamic:

- How are you behaving?
- How are you feeling?
- What do you see?
- What do you hear?
- What do you notice is important about the situation?
- What is important to you?

120 *Framing of experience*

- Adopt the meta-position (step out from directly associating and dis-associate from an analytical base) to reflect on this stage of the exercise.
- What can you learn from this position?

3 Adopt the second position and associate with the stakeholder:

- How are you behaving?
- How are you feeling?
- What do you see?
- What do you hear?
- What do you notice is important about the situation?
- What do you believe about the situation?
- What is important to you?
- Adopt the meta-position to reflect on this stage of the exercise.
- What is there for you to learn?
- How has your perception changed?

4 Adopt the third position and associate with the role of independent observer:

- How are the actors behaving?
- How are the actors feeling?
- What beliefs do they each appear to be using?
- What is important to each of them?
- Adopt the meta-position
- What is there for you to learn?
- How has your perception changed?

5 Stay in the meta-position bringing your new learning and perceptions with you.
6 Reflect on all three positions. How has your initial model of perception changed?
7 What will your new attitude be?
8 What will your new behavioural strategy be?
9 Test and future pace. This involves going back to the first position in the social context and fully associating with it using your 'new' resources.
10 Step out and back into the meta-position. Reflect on your feelings and beliefs.

This is a very simple yet effective technique to be able to build an understanding of:

- The reality frame being used by others to make sense of the situation under review.
- The beliefs that are supporting the frame.
- The values that are supporting the beliefs.

Framing of experience 121

- The positive intention behind the frame.
- The behavioural strategies they are employing
- Their general motivations

If we think about Karen and if we imagine she can internalize perceptual position mapping as a change leadership strategy we can appreciate the ontological, behavioural, cognitive and emotional flexibility she can access as a change leader in such a situation.

Ontological flexibility: She can pace multiple reality frames. She is open to adjusting her own. She is less rigid in her understanding of the situation. She is respectful and understanding and tolerant towards the reality frames held by others.
Behavioural flexibility: She can behave in a way that encourages the expression of alternative reality frames within a change meeting. She can adopt an open and relaxed manner which invites dialogue.
Cognitive flexibility: She can choose to reflect on her own meta-programmes. She can pace the meta-programmes, values and beliefs held by others effectively.
Emotional flexibility: She can future pace change leadership encounters with stakeholders who hold different reality frames and self-programme COACH state in advance of these meetings. She will be emotionally familiar with the emotions and general mindsets of others and can design her soft skills strategies for managing the encounters.

Each person, we assume, will be emotionally attached to their own model. They will most likely try to defend and advance their own model. Also, they are all, we assume, authentic constructions, each person holds these with integrity. In NLP terms, we would say that each person has a positive intention behind their attitudes and behaviours. We can also add that in the moment each person decides on their world view based upon the resources available to them at the time. So, for Karen, we would invite her to respect the reality model of each person, to pace their experience implicit in the symbolism of their model. This approach involves Karen adopting an empathetic and understanding attitude towards her stakeholders rather than a judgemental and defensive stance.

All the above, at first attempt, take time and practice. However, after a while you will literally imbed the technique into your cerebral muscles and use it unconsciously and this level of emotional intelligence will greatly enhance your capability as a change leader. There is no guarantee that this approach will ensure that the stakeholders agree to reframe in line with the frames held by the change leader; however, there is a far greater prospect that psychological safety will be created and the diffusion model of change leadership enhanced leading to collaborative dialogue and, perhaps, the emergence of a shared reality frame that enables a basis of coherent stakeholder action.

122 *Framing of experience*

The change leader may use NLP techniques such as perceptual mapping to authentically engage with the reality frames held by others and establish an understanding of stakeholders' emotional and cognitive states. This strategy will enable access to COACH state and the avoidance of the related CRASH state that often results from conflicting models of the world in an atmosphere of low tolerance.

The change leader cannot avoid the challenge of every day reframing as a meaning-maker, as a map maker. The requirement is to provide change leaders like Karen with the cognitive, emotional, and behavioural flexibility to do these activities competently.

Framing of experience

As we experience the empirical world, we distil an endless stream of sense data. Through the use of language we structure the symbolic composition of selected sensory experiences into 'experiential frames' (Bandler & Grinder, 1982). These frames can be thought of as metaphors, i.e., as with a portrait in a frame. Our symbolic constructions are akin to paintings we frame and store in our memories. We attribute meanings to these framed experiences and these meanings drive our attitudes and, thus, our behaviours. This means that how we frame experience can be correlated with the social results we experience through our interactions. For example, if one's early framing of educational experience was one which suggested you were not academic and, thus, not suited to advanced scholarly study then one may select an attitude that generates behaviour which avoids situations where academic study is required. One may also frame academics as, somehow, not practical people who have no role to play in one's life. This kind of framing of experience has a limiting effect not only on the person doing the framing but also, perhaps, on others who are influenced by this person. It is important for rapport-building purposes that we are sensitive to the frames through which we make sense of and operate in the world around us, in particular, for rapport purposes, the social world. If we can critically reflect on our framed experience and its content and functions then we can intervene and socially reconstruct our frames of reference, change our associated attitudes and generated behavioural strategies and thus influence our social results.

Reframing

An important activity for change leaders to master is the practice of reframing. This is defined by O'Connor and Seymour (1990pp234) as *"Changing the frame of reference around a statement to give it another meaning"*. In chapter 4 I discussed both content and context reframing. For now I wish to consider reframing as a change leadership strategy. Change leadership involves reframing processes. To be blunt, if a person cannot collaborate with others to create an atmosphere of psychological safety which leads to a group COACH state enabling a reframing project as a basis for coherent group action then they have failed as a change leader. The process of perceptual position mapping helps build the internal resources the change leader requires to enable a reframing process at both an individual and group level. However, it is the sum of the multiple parts of our model for building psychological safety that influences change leadership efforts at enabling a reframe in others.

If we revisit the case of Karen as a potential change leader we can see that she can identify with the reality frames held by the key stakeholders and the beliefs and values supporting these. We know that she can prepare herself for the reframing process by pre-programming strategies that will provide her with behavioural, cognitive, ontological, and emotional flexibility. We also know that in NLP terms we can rely on 'The Law of Requisite Variety' to support Karen in her leadership efforts. As previously discussed The Law of Requisite Variety implies that the person with the greatest behavioural, cognitive, ontological, and emotional flexibility within the social system will prevail. If we then add to Karen's change leadership toolkit the additional soft skills of our model, she will be adequately prepared for the reframing process. A simple yet powerful re-framing technique is the A to E method which is explained below.

Phase A = **Adversity** event

Let us say the change leader is to host an event where they are to deliver an important speech and they are experiencing a lack of confidence which triggers negative emotion.

Phase B = **Belief** system

People often hold limiting beliefs about the negative situation that are counter productive and reduce clear thinking. The belief in this case may be that the change leader believes that their audience will not be receptive to their message.

Phase C = **Consequences** of the irrational belief

The belief then functions like a self-fulfilling prophecy generating irrational and limiting thoughts which produce negative consequences. The change leader is creating these anxieties through their initial framing of how they believe their audience will respond, yet they have no way in advance of knowing how they will respond. Research indicates that the expectation one establishes in one's mindset of others can and often does manifest in reality (Dweck, 2006).

Phase D = **Disputing** irrational thoughts and beliefs

The aim of this phase is to challenge the irrational beliefs in a clear and direct manner. This is important to replace the negative and unrealistic thinking with a more realistic and adaptive appraisal of challenging situations. This is the opportunity to re-frame. If the change leader connects with one's internal coach (internal part) they can experiment with different assumptions as regards the speech:

124 *Framing of experience*

1 *"This is a great opportunity for me to really connect with my colleagues."*
2 *"I know that my colleagues will have doubts and that's understandable; this is my chance to share my concerns too and my feelings of optimism."*
3 *"It's natural to be concerned and even cynical when you are worried about the future; my job is to acknowledge these feelings in my colleagues and help them work through the shared challenge. I am so looking forward to doing this."*
4 *"All my colleagues are coming from a positive place; they want what I want which is to be successful; they will be hoping that I can tell them how we are going to do this. This is a great privilege for me."*

When you play around with these reframing strategies, it is helpful to adopt the perceptual positioning strategy to experience triple perceptual description (first, second and third, perceptual positions) which will bring about a state change. This gives you confidence that the group state can and will change depending on your own state.

Phase E = **Effects** of changing one's interpretation of a situation

In this phase, the client is more open and more approachable to new solutions they use to react to the situation. They may feel optimistic, eager to deliver and confident that they can connect with their audience in a very open and resourceful way and they will do the same by return.

You can also practice this technique with the support of a colleague who acts as your coach using the following process.

1 The coach asks their partner to identify a challenging situation they have been concerned about.
2 The coach asks their partner to describe the **adversity** event using sensory based questions in as much detail as possible.
3 The coach then elicits from their partner accounts of their limiting **beliefs**.
4 The coach then asks their partner to describe the **consequences** which result from these beliefs in as much detail as possible.
5 Then the coach will invite their partner to **dispute** the negative and limiting thought and reframe the event and the beliefs in far more resourceful ways.
6 Finally, the coach asks their partner about the **effect** of the new belief structure when they think about the activating event.

The participant will sharpen his or her skills of self-awareness and will learn a method of how to positively influence his or her state. This ability will help the participant to steer their team successfully through difficulties and challenges, including conflict, diversity, and inclusion issues within the team.

Concluding thoughts

Change leaders, according to Alvesson and Sveningsson (2015), need to engage thoughtfully in the active process of everyday reframing of the values, attitudes, beliefs and behaviours they expect others to model. NLP, as demonstrated above, provides methodologies that enable such a process. For corporate NLP trainers, change is often concerned with transforming the symbolic nature of the meaning systems that managers employ to make sense of their environments. This is a significant finding of Alvesson and Sveningsson who developed their idea of everyday reframing of social reality through the modelling of desirable attitudes and behaviours. This is a very personal and introspective process for managers. It stands in sharp contrast to technical change that managers can, in the main, stand apart from in a very calculating and overtly rational way, characteristic of the transmission model of change leadership. Change leaders need a framework of action-orientated methods that they can internalize and practice daily to stimulate reframing processes in others that do not create a space for toxic symbolism and the associated narratives that undermine change projects. NLP provides such a model.

References

Alvesson, M. and Sveningsson, S. (2015) *Changing Organizational Culture*, Routledge.
Bandler, R. and Grinder, J. (1975) *The Structure of Magic, V1*, Science and Behaviour Books.
Bandler, R. and Grinder, J. (1982) *Reframing*, Real People Press.
Dweck, C.S. (2006) *MINDSET: How You Can Fulfil your Potential*, Robinson.
O'Connor, J. and Seymour, J. (1990) *Introducing NLP: Neuro Linguistic Programming*, Mandala.

13 Caretaking and guiding

Introduction

In this chapter I will address the foundations of a change leader's role which involves caretaking and guiding change participants' experience of the change work that is to unfold. Guiding involves directing change subjects along a journey of generative change from one state to another, whilst caretaking involves providing a safe and supportive environment for this process to emerge successfully. This means that change leaders must insist that the venues they plan to use as coaching containers are environmentally sound, psychologically safe and have a physical set-up that enables generative dialogue. Change leaders should not perceive these details as pedestrian, or factors that should be addressed by others. Change leaders must be able to meta-reflect on their own states and the energy they are giving off and the generative field around them that they are co-creating with the participants.

NLP and psychological safety

The main reason that NLP can help build an atmosphere of psychological safety in a group or between two people is that its originators modelled the work and practices of leading psychotherapists. Bandler and Grinder (1975) wanted to understand how these psychotherapists achieved their successful change outcomes when working with clients which included family groups. Now before you think… '*oh dear; therapy*' please bear in mind that the work of Rogers (1965) into client centred therapy heavily influenced the founders and early pioneers of the OD movement (French & Bell, 1999) and OD developers such as Merry and Brown (1987) also used Perls (1973) Gestalt Therapy to examine neurosis as an organizational dysfunction. Whenever you get people coming together over time you generate localized cultures and within cultural groups you experience psychological challenges that are susceptible to therapeutic approaches.

Bandler and Grinder (1975) identify the ability of the therapists they were modelling to build rapport with their clients as a core competence behind successful change work. As we will discover in Chapter 14 rapport

Caretaking and guiding 127

involves creating a generative field between people based on trust and acceptance.

As an essential element of both caretaking and guiding, the NLP trainer is taught to acutely respect rapport-building processes. They are very sensitive to the energy they transmit and generate; to the setting for a client meeting or a training session; the presentation of self; the meta-programmes they use; the spatial arrangement of a training venue; the environmental factors that affect emotional states; and the meta-messages that can be toxic if not managed effectively. They are also sensitive to the potential influence of both mirror neurons and emotional contagions (Hatfield et al., 2014) being generated by influential participants who may be in CRASH state and who may act as role models for other participants. We match instinctively the behaviour of the significant other.

Emotional contagion involves one person's emotions and related behaviours directly triggering similar emotions and behaviours in other people. When people unconsciously mirror their colleague's expressions of emotion, they come to feel reflections of those colleague's emotions. They model their colleagues. This process is also enabled by the idea of the 'significant other' as developed by Mead (1934). When we have significant others in our social field we are susceptible to unconsciously modelling their emotions, cognitions, behaviours, values, and beliefs. The NLP trainer is very sensitive to these ideas and processes and will use techniques to 'disrupt' the patterns if they are toxic to the wider field.

A technique that is incredibly simple is to involve the audience in participative exercises. It is understood that emotion follows motion. Simply inviting your audience to participate in an exercise which involves movement and introspection can disrupt the emergence of a non-resourceful energy field. For example, you could use a powerful NLP exercise called 'the getting to know you exercise'. This NLP pattern involves the following steps.

The trainer will invite everyone to choose a conversational partner for two minutes. Each participant will take one minute to explain to the other:

- Who they are; this includes where they were born, where they grew up, where they live and, of course, their name
- What they do; this includes professionally and whatever they wish to share socially
- What they want from the course
- What they want from the other person
- What they are most proud of

The conversational partner guides the question and answer sequence. The guide is to deliberately match the body language and posture of their conversational partner and backtrack with them thus pacing their experience and demonstrating their attentiveness.

128 *Caretaking and guiding*

The trainer blows a horn and that is the signal for the pairings to break and find new conversational partners. This exercise is completed three times.

This kind of pattern interrupt has the potential of distracting the cynics and engaging with the wider audience and establishing the basis for a generative field. The great therapists understood that this getting to know you process was a fundamental strategy to create the conditions required for successful change work.

Toxic meta-messages

When building a climate of trust, a significant challenge for change leaders is managing the corrosive influence of toxic symbolism generated by meta-messages gone wrong. This is significant because it naturally involves confronting activities enacted by managers which are incongruent with the espoused intentions of the change project. In NLP terms, we call these variables meta-messages which can be defined as messages conveyed to others either consciously or unconsciously through non-verbal communications. For example, a manager claims, verbally, to support the change programme whilst shaking their head sideways as they talk, or delivering extensive monologues when they are supposed to be actively trying to generate dialogue.

Meta-messages are messages about other messages, usually expressed through nonverbal cues. A meta-message can reveal the difference between what a person says and what they mean. Meta-messages are unconscious expressions. For change leaders, being aware of meta-messages helps to understand the audience and to ensure that they, themselves, do not communicate messages that are not congruent about the change programme. Being aware of the potential of meta-messages to creep into our presentations of self as a credible change leader is very important regarding caretaking and guiding.

Other ways that we send out meta-messages are through the process of tonal marking where we underscore key words or phrases with voice tones that are not congruent with the verbalized message. Many meta-messages are delivered using very subtle cues and some are rather blunt. The way a manager sits in a meeting can convey a meta-message regarding their commitment to the change project, and the physiology, thinking styles, voice tone, breathing patterns and whom they choose to sit beside, can all function as meta-messages that reveal the nature of relationships, identifications, and levels of commitment regarding the sponsor's change agenda.

A particularly toxic symbol that can be mediated through the meta-message is silence. If change leaders, or rather expected change leaders, do not regularly talk up the change programme, this is a meta-message. If they simply communicate with a regular voice tone with little enthusiasm for the alleged message of support, this is a meta-message. If they arrive consistently late for team meetings, fail to meet deadlines or deliver tasks, then these are meta-messages. If they do not follow up agenda items with change teams, then this is a meta-message. Can you imagine these things occurring during a change project and the mini narratives that morph into toxic symbols that change participants co-author? I can.... I have fully experienced such a dynamic. I can assure you that whilst senior managers derive an immediate gain of emotional safety and false harmony through blindsiding these kinds of meta-messages, they are doing great harm to the organization's capacity for change and self-renewal. Caretaking involves managing the toxic impact of meta-messages.

NLP greatly enhances our sensory acuity and, thus, our ability to notice and read meta-messages. For change leaders to be successful, they need to communicate the idea of meta-messages throughout the management community and build an atmosphere where they can be identified for what they are and confronted and addressed. This is not an easy thing to do. It is a leadership act involving both caretaking and guiding processes. Yes, leaders will claim that it is important to maintain harmony in a team and confrontation is a bad thing for team spirit. NLP helps us explore the substance of these beliefs, to identify the weaknesses in them and the secondary gains produced by holding on to these on the part of managers in charge of change projects. NLP also provides a philosophy through which we can filter our emotional states when we recognize meta-messages which are manifesting as toxic symbols and hurting the change programme.

Building a coaching container

Part of the role as a caretaker is to generate a coaching container within which people can feel confident in their relationship with you as the leader, and with the rest of the group, so that they may express themselves without fear of any attack on their sense of self. Therefore, a meeting room is no longer a meeting room, instead it is to be understood as a creative space through which difficult feelings may be held and channelled safely. This is a style of leadership that involves building a relationship through which the lead influencers act as caretakers of the environment that their audience is to interact within. This involves accepting our responsibility to calibrate, pace, elicit and lead others into a state of psychological safety within which they feel no threat to their established identities. This involves providing a safe and supportive environment.

Managing our energy

When, as change leaders, we bring people together, we generate a presence in the room. This presence has a significant influence upon the wider generative field that resonates between the full audience. A generative field can be understood as an energy that is mirrored between an audience and which enables each person to enter and hold a highly resourceful state. The model COACH state is a good example of the mindset that the participants should enter once a generative field has been established.

130 *Caretaking and guiding*

If the change leader is perhaps over-anxious about meeting and engaging with their audience, they may be slipping into CRASH state. If this is the case, then the energy they will give off will most probably be unsettling and incongruent with their actual intentions. This negative energy can seep into the unconscious minds of audience members who will model the CRASH state being actualized by the change leader. This process is known in psychology as an emotional contagion and was developed by Hatfield et al. (2014). As previously discussed, people literally catch the emotional states and energies from other people through unconscious modelling. Thus, it is incumbent upon the change leader as a guide and as a caretaker to critically reflect on their emotional, cognitive, and behavioural states and adjust these if they find themselves moving away from COACH to CRASH state.

Building COACH state

For change leaders engaged in building a climate of psychological safety this process of managing one's mindset and privileging COACH state and avoiding CRASH state cannot be underestimated.

Robert Dilts of NLPU along with his colleague Stephen Gilligan developed the acronym COACH and CRASH to enable clients and NLP trainers and coaches to identify discreet emotional states that were generating attitudes and behaviours that were either enabling positive or negative experiences. The method is straightforward. One simply identifies an experience they have had that generates, by association of thought, the state of mind implicit in each COACH state variable. For example, a time in one's life when one felt really connected to a project or to an audience. They anchor these experiences by associating them with a personal symbol, then link them together under the heading of COACH (described below) and when the person needs these resources they simply 'collapse' the anchors one after the other to experience COACH state.

Once each person has built their chain of anchors and internalized their own COACH construct then before each meeting change leaders can invite all participants to enter COACH state through group participation in an exercise led by the facilitator for the meeting. In my experience, when this is undertaken without inhibition and with sincerity, the climate for the meeting is creative, and generative. One does feel psychologically safe because I have stimulated a state of mind that is Connected with the project and the people in the room, Open to the ideas and thinking strategies of others and open to introspection and trust, Attentive to the needs of others; feeling Centred and confident and, finally, bringing my full sense of self to the meeting so that the others know that they can trust me to Hold challenging feelings.

Stacking emotional states

When building a coaching container, we are involved in the process of stacking emotional states on top of each other. For example, we may stack

Caretaking and guiding 131

negative emotional states on top of each other and end up in CRASH state, which is a super toxic negative state or mind set. CRASH stands for:

C: Contracted: feelings of isolation, lack of connection with the organization and one's colleagues.

R: Reactive: not having time to reflect and survey one's culture and work-based events and learn and share the learning from reflective experiences.

A: Action paralysis: struggling with information overload due to difficult relationships and toxic emotions.

S: Separate: feeling alone and lacking in trusting relationships within the workplace, lack of perception regarding the vision and mission of the organization.

H: Hurting: feeling undervalued, underwhelmed, regretting not having the chance to really make a difference at work.

Many management cultures are in CRASH state and simply do not know how to transform this unproductive state of mind and enjoy far more productive team-based relationships. NLP rapport-building skills can enable the smooth transformation of individual and group states from CRASH state to the more productive COACH state.

If the change leader is in COACH state then they will be able to access their unconscious mind and explore the characteristics of their shadow self and review the ways in which it influences their emotions, behaviours, and cognitions and, thus, the social strategies that generate their results. This is a safe technique that presents no threat to the public version of the change leader and it is a technique that is easily modelled and self-administered. When you are in state of internal rapport you are in a high performing state. When you are in this state of mind other people sense this and if you then build rapport with them you have both internal and external rapport, and this is a very powerful resource state to be in.

You can programme your mind to adopt a meta-programme that privileges COACH state orientations as a change leader. This involves building your COACH state. The operating principle behind building COACH state involves identifying a unique prior experience from either the first or second position that generates each specific element and anchoring this against a symbol of your choice. By firing each anchor, you can release each resourceful state or specific elements and bring these with you into any social situation that you feel would benefit from these. The following example is a typical exercise developed by Robert Dilts which is based upon the NLP techniques of perceptual positioning, anchoring, state elicitation and somatic reinforcement

Exercise building COACH state

The trainer is to invite a participant to join them on stage.

1   In pairs take turns at telling each other a story of a time in your life that was memorable for you that you can associate with each 'element' of COACH state. The guide is to elicit rich sensory descriptions.

132 *Caretaking and guiding*

2 Invite the performer to think of an anchor for each experiential reference they design for COACH state.
3 Invite the participant to create a somatic gesture (a physical sign such as a specific hand movement) for each element of their circle of success.
4 Invite the performer to stand up and agree a working space on the floor that both of you can operate from.
5 Invite the performer to visualize a circle on the ground and project the anchor into the circle and build a chain of anchors.
6 Each circle is called the participant's circle of excellence.
7 The NLP trainer is to invite the participant to enter their circle of excellence and fully associate with this element of their COACH state.
8 After completing one direct association, the participant leaves their circle of excellence and steps in to their meta-position to 'shake off' the experience and prepare for the next association.
9 The trainer is to prompt descriptive accounts of a sensory nature from the storyteller as they directly associate with each element of COACH state from within their circle of excellence.
10 Ask the participant to identify social situations going forward, or in the past where this resource would have been useful.
11 They are to calibrate their partner and support their performance with signs of encouragement.
12 The trainer is also to match the body language and voice tone and speed of their partner.
13 The performer is then to be invited to collapse each anchor and, in their circles, fully associate with the experiential COACH state.
14 The final stage involves the participant returning to their meta-position and reflecting on each of their COACH state anchors and their somatic gestures.

COACH state audit

A COACH state audit simply involves moving to a meta-thinking state and critically self-reflecting on one's state of mind by asking the following questions:

Connected: Do I feel connected to my co-learners and my trainers?

Centred: Do I feel confident that I belong in this social space and that it is psychologically safe for me?

Open: Do I feel open to the ideas of others, curious and secure in being open about my own thought?

Attentive: Am I attentive to the needs of my co learners, trainers and the learnings being generated?

Holding: Can I hold onto to difficult feelings in a resourceful way?

If your answers are mainly yes, then you can confidently say you are in COACH state. And you can most definitely feedback critical observations to your significant others from COACH state if you are being authentic regarding the positive intentions lying behind your feedback data. The challenge with this dynamic involves the ability of the significant other in building a climate or culture of psychological safety that enables this dynamic to emerge. As previously stated, in NLP terms we call this generating a coaching container; a meeting room or a training room or an office becomes a dedicated space to hold challenging feelings and to express these in constructive ways confident that they will be received absent of defensive routines and with a sincere welcome.

Another key element of building a coaching container is thinking through the spatial content of the venue being used. Robert Dilts calls this process 'psychogeography'.

Psychogeography

Robert Dilts (2003, p. 9) states that "*Psychogeography refers to the influence that micro geographical arrangements and relationships exert on people's psychological processes and interpersonal interactions.*" Thus, if you want to build rapport with an individual, a group of two, or a group of more than two then how you arrange the room is very important. Also, how sensitive you are to cultural norms regarding the protective space people expect to be respected around them has implications for rapport building. If you stand alongside someone then this can help build feelings of support. If you can sit next to someone this indicates togetherness and a sense of acceptance. If you sit directly facing someone this could indicate a contest. If you sit opposite yet distant this can indicate resistance between the interactors. The dynamics involved in group formations also impact considerably on the degree of rapport one can achieve. Thus, sensitivity to spatial arrangements is important regarding rapport-building processes.

Nancy Dixon (1996), who has generated an enormous amount of insight into dialogical practices, advances the idea of conversational circles as a core psychogeography technique. As circles of chairs have no starting point and no end and no corners then the group will feel a reduction in hierarchical symbolism and perhaps feel safer. It may be the case that people feel a little strange at first in a circle; however, through time they will start to demonstrate their involvement as they adjust their body language, heighten their sensory acuity, and actively engage in a dialogue.

If you, as a change leader, bring an audience together in a classroom-style format, using PowerPoint as the main medium, this is fine if all you want is to deliver a personal monologue. It does not create a generative field though; it disables dialogue and it is unlikely that your audience will feel connected to your case for change or psychologically safe.

Concluding thoughts

This chapter has considered the role of change leaders building a climate which values acutely recognizing and making space for acknowledging the

134   *Caretaking and guiding*

authenticity of all individuals involved in the change space. It also has paid attention to the identity of change leaders as caretakers and guides in that they have responsibilities to ensure that the environment provides a supportive structure for change teams to operate within. Thinking about our own states and the energy we generate and the way in which rooms are organized and psychological safety is built up are very important issues that, if left unattended, will most definitely undermine the change leadership process. NLP pays attention to these details and offers a well-formed model for managing them effectively.

We must first practice NLP on ourselves and this means being open to the way our own maps act as filters and barriers to collaborating with others. Can I build rapport with someone whose map conflicts with my own? Can I tolerate well-intentioned interventions into my map? For me these two skills are at the very heart of NLP practice. The absence of these simply undermines my core identity as an NLP developer. I try to be the best version of myself and I will continue to do so. The next chapter will address a model of rapport building

References

Bandler, R. and Grinder, J. (1975) *The Structure of Magic*, Science and Behaviour Books Inc.

Dilts, R. (2003) *From Coach to Awakener*, Meta Publications.

Dixon, N. (1996) *Perspectives on Dialogue*, Center for Creative Leadership.

French, W. L. and Bell, C. H. (1999) *Organizational Development*, 6th edn, Prentice Hall.

Hatfield, E., Bensman, L., Thornton, D. P., and Rapson, L. R. (2014) *New Perspectives on Emotional Contagion: A Review of Classic and Recent Research on Facial Mimicry and Contagion*, Interpersona.

Mead, G. H. (1934) *Mind, Self and Society, from the Standpoint of a Social Behaviourist*, University of Chicago Press.

Merry, U. and Brown, L. G. (1987) *The Neurotic Behaviour of Organizations*, Gardner Press.

Perls, F. (1973) *The Gestalt Approach: An Eye Witness to Therapy*, Science and Behaviour Books.

Rogers, R. C. (1965) *Client-Centered Therapy*, ABE Books.

14 A model of rapport building

This chapter will consider the subject of rapport which is central to NLP practice as well as being the guiding principle for change leadership efforts. Rapport is, arguably, the magical ingredient that is at the base of all successful relationships and, thus, is seen by NLP trainers and practitioners as a vitally important skill. The early developers and pioneers behind the birth of the NLP movement spent considerable time modelling excellent examples of rapport strategies. They modelled the rapport-building skills of world class therapists who achieved consistent success at guiding clients through complex personal and family change.

Much of the literature concerning change management leadership describes fault lines which undermine a change programme as being connected to resistance on the part of stakeholder groups. This negative identity creates a problematic tension between those who support the change programme and those who do not. NLP offers a paradigm that disrupts this kind of them versus us thinking. NLP advances the view that *'resistance is a sign of poor rapport'*. Thus, NLP practitioners accept responsibility for their social results. If change participants are resisting our leadership efforts and are framing our communications in ways that are disabling the realization of our intentions, then for NLP practitioners this is a product of our own inability to build rapport. We must reflect on the social strategies we are employing and use the feedback constructively to adopt a different approach to build rapport. This type of thinking is known in organizational studies as reflective practice and NLP practitioners are, by definition, reflective practitioners. In this chapter I shall survey NLP techniques and ideas which can enable rapport-building processes to emerge as significant change leadership skill sets.

Defining rapport

Rapport is defined as low resistance between two or more individuals which enables alignment of values, attitudes, beliefs, and behaviours. Rapport is a magical dynamic which enables influencing processes and winning friends. People do tend to like people who are like themselves. This is how Dilts and DeLozier (2000, p. 1051) frame rapport.

136 *A model of rapport building*

> *One of the most important relational skills in NLP is the ability to estab-lish rapport with others. Rapport involves building trust, harmony, and cooperation in a relationship. 'Harmonious mutual understanding,' 'agree-ment,' being 'in tune' and 'in accord,' are some of the words used to describe the process and or the state of being in rapport with another.*

These two NLP pioneers also cite *Webster's Dictionary* which defines rap-port as a state of 'sympathy which permits influence or communication'. They make the point that the quality of information you can exchange with others is dependent on the degree of rapport you have with them. In their book *Introducing NLP* O'Connor and Seymour (1990, p. 234) define rapport as: "*The process of establishing and maintaining a relationship of mutual trust and understanding between two or more people.*"

Dilts and DeLozier (2000, p. 1051) employ the metaphor of a dance to advance their definition of rapport. They position rapport as an improvised process that is nonlinear, that is, in fact, a creative matching of the rhythm of mind, body and soul. When one is trying to build rapport, one is subtly dancing with the world view of the other, a process that is called 'pacing' in NLP. Pacing enables rapport. The aim is not to inculcate the world view of the other, rather when building rapport, one is trying to respect the world view of the other and to understand it so that the channels may open between people.

Rapport can also be defined as '*the quality of a relationship that results in mutual trust and responsiveness*'. Rapport refers to a form of relationship between people that enables mutually beneficial sense making. Rapport is the cohesive element in social relations that enables social bonding between people. When one is in a state of rapport with another person, or with a group, it is an experience that can be considered as being in tune with others. Rather like the frequency of a radio station, when building rapport, we are literally tuning in to the other's wave length. Rapport is an essential part of society's structural and cultural dynamics. It is difficult to conceive of a cohesive and stable society or culture in the absence of rapport.

Rapport as a performance indicator

The strength of rapport between two people can define the quality of the relationship they have with each other. In many ways the absence or strength of rapport established between key stakeholders during change projects func-tions as a key performance indicator. A lack of rapport, or very weak rap-port, should be a cause for considerable concern amongst the change leadership group. Rapport involves an incremental social process that opens channels for generative dialogue.

Building rapport with key stakeholders is a critical part of the leadership process. There is little doubt that an inability to both understand what rap-port is and to consciously build rapport with key stakeholders is a fault line

A model of rapport building   137

that runs through change projects. In a management career spanning 25 years I cannot think of a time when I received training regarding rapport building. The reason for this, I think, is that rapport is simply not considered as a key leadership skill. It is a social skill that is often expected at a level of unconscious awareness and yet it is, arguably, one of the most important skill sets a change leader in an organization can possess. To be in a state of rapport one requires empathy and curiosity in relation to others and their perspectives.

Building rapport is a social skill that we all have the capacity to develop. Rapport can be defined as '_the ability to elicit positive responses from the other_'. This ability is an essential competence required to establish you in a leadership role. Rapport builds trust and strengthens relationships which, during periods of intense change, are critical human resources.

Dale Carnegie (1936) asserted that the ability to build rapport and manage productive relationships was key to business success. Rapport is the aim of NLP. It is the meta-guiding principle of NLP. Beyond the practice of NLP, the ability of the individual to function competently and with success in the broader social world is hugely influenced by their ability to establish rapport with people.

Rapport is a magical dynamic which, as Carnegie (1936) said, enables influencing processes and winning friends. An essential performance indicator for rapport is when we can see and hear two or more people being comfortable in engaging in dialogue. Rapport involves matching the body language, voice tone and representational systems of those we are trying to engage with. Leaders will struggle to lead unless they can build rapport with their followers. This means that they must develop their communication skills, including matching the way in which different people perceive the world.

Matching strategies also include matching body language, voice tone, breathing rates and thinking strategies. It can also involve matching the clothes we wear and the cultural norms of an organization. Leading successful change is only made possible because, by adopting a leadership role, we can convince others that it is in their interest to engage in reflective and generative dialogue to review culture at work with a view to changing or transforming aspects of its dynamics. This can only start from a position of rapport.

It's in our DNA

As we develop as human beings we unconsciously develop our rapport-building skills. What happens is that through time we bond culturally with people who are like ourselves. This is one of the universal principles of human nature; people like people who are like themselves. If this is the case, then the ability to establish rapport with another person is critical to getting on with that person and eliciting their support for our activities. As previously stated in change management terms, be it at the level of the individual, the group or inter-group, the ability of the change manager to establish rapport is a critical determining success factor.

138 *A model of rapport building*

Rapport as a bridge towards dialogue

Rapport, for me, is the bridge that takes us to a state of 'generative dialogue', which is the essential ingredient to enable successful collaboration and the leverage of the collective intelligence of a team. When one is in a state of active rapport with others one can access a state of generative dialogue; this is defined by Isaacs (1999) as '*the art of thinking together*'. Rapport induces cohesiveness and a readiness for joint decision making and action, it ensures that working relations are fluid and coherent. People who are in rapport tend to enjoy the experience of socializing together and, thus, they have an emotional investment in protecting and maintaining their rapport. It should be clear that the ability to build rapport with others and then maintain it over time is a highly valuable skill set. The learning of this skill set followed by its successful practical application is a significant aim of NLP as a body of learning and practice.

Collaborative change is only possible if there are leaders who are capable of building rapport with followers. It follows, logically, that the practice of generative dialogue on both vertical and horizontal levels throughout the change community is a critical part of the successful change mix. Dialogue aims to release the 'authentic voice' that we all have inside of us. Dialogue aims to enable change participants to adopt open, differentiated, and integrated perspectives. It is through dialogue that meanings are constructed and flow; so, it is only through dialogue that meanings can be changed and, thus, change interactions must be enabled through dialogical processes.

Rapport-building model

NLP developers have identified the critical processes involved in establishing rapport with people. These processes do not have a hierarchy of importance in relation to one another. They must be blended together by the practitioner to be effective. Although they do have a natural linear order there is a series of logical stages for each process to be actualized by the practitioner to establish rapport. Though, once rapport is established one would enact the different processes at different times depending on the nature of the symbolic interactions taking place between people. Figure 14.1 provides an illustration of the main process categories involved in rapport building.

Calibration

Calibration is defined by Dilts and DeLozier (2000, p. 137) as "*the process of learning how to read another person's responses in an ongoing interaction*". To calibrate involves developing sensory acuity which involves the ability to be very sensitive to the physiological and tonal cues that signify the state of mind of the individual or group. So, calibration involves the conscious process of reading the state of the other, and sensory acuity is the practice of refining one's calibration skills to the level of micro observation.

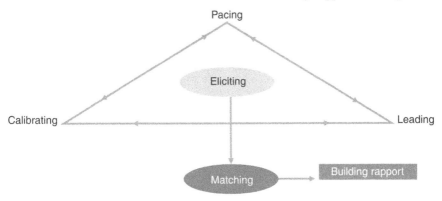

Figure 14.1 A model of rapport processes

To attain rapport, one needs to be able to calibrate the state of the other with skill. This process involves accurately assessing the mental state that the other is in through assessing their verbal and physiological cues. By studying accessing cues, such as body posture, movements, voice tone, breathing rate, and sensory systems employed, one can obtain a reasonably accurate picture of the state of mind someone is in. This process of calibration means that one can select the appropriate behavioural, emotional or cognitive strategy to match the state of the other person. You may choose a strategy which aims to pace the experience of the other.

Unconscious calibration

When people are in a group they will form social relationships with each other that will determine the dynamics of the group. There will be leaders of varying influence who will influence the group during the interaction. Often group members will unconsciously calibrate not only you as the proactive rapport builder but also their peers and, in particular, the significant others within the group. Their unconscious mind will interpret micro signals which function as meta-messages amongst the group and which stimulate attitude formation. An important part of rapport building is the ability to track through active calibration the meta-messages being unconsciously generated within the group and, if possible, being able to disrupt these by breaking the emerging group state and eliciting a different state that is favourable to your agenda. This may involve pacing and then leading which can also involve adopting characteristics that are not necessarily part of one's normal repertoire. In many ways the skills used in calibrating and then leading a group are akin to the skills of an actor.

Calibrated loops

Dilts and Delozier (2000, p. 140) define calibrated loops as *"an unconscious pattern of communication in which behavioural cues coming from one person*

140 *A model of rapport building*

trigger specific responses in another person". The critical nature of calibration loops is that they serve to reproduce unconscious behavioural patterns in others. They act as stimulus to these behaviours. Obviously, if the generative behaviour is deemed as positive, calibrated loops are to be welcomed; however, if they generate negative behavioural strategies that disrupt rapport then they must be disrupted and changed.

Matching

The saying *'people like people who are like themselves'* can be taken as a generalization about an important aspect of human nature. Human beings use culture to produce shared meanings, values, assumptions, beliefs, attitudes, habits, and behaviours that bind a group together and which provide social stability. This phenomenon has been studied extensively by anthropologists and sociologists and is called the 'cultural paradigm'. The existence of the cultural paradigm as the expressive engine of a cultural group is generally accepted as a universal cultural theme running through humanity. People also share meta-programmes which is an NLP term for the cultural themes or rules that guide the thought processes and sense making of individuals and groups within a particular cultural context. If you try to build a relationship with someone and if you hold a contrasting meta-programme and cultural paradigm, then it may prove difficult for you to build rapport. Therefore, one has to match aspects of identities in order to put a person or group at ease and to create a dynamic where their channels are open to your suggestions and ideas. What you are trying to do is to establish something in common symbolically between you. You are trying to break the potential for mismatching which can disrupt rapport-building processes. According to Dilts and Delozier (2000, p. 698) matching is:

> *An interactive skill, matching refers to the process of reflecting or feeding back the cognitive or behavioural patterns of another person; for example, sitting in a similar posture, using the same gestures, speaking in a similar voice tone are examples of behavioural matching.*

Thus, matching involves adopting similar body posture, voice tone, and representational systems to the other. If you match effectively you will act as an unconscious mirror to the other who is more likely to relax with you and enter into a state of rapport. You must not be too obvious in your matching strategy or you run the risk of making the other self-conscious and uncomfortable. You can subtly match by adopting similar physiology but not, necessarily, identical. For example, if someone is an auditory sense maker and they nod their head in rhythm with their speech tempo you may gently tap your finger in correspondence. Or if someone sits with their legs crossed one over the other you may sit with your legs partially crossed. This is known as 'cross-over mirroring'.

A model of rapport building 141

Pacing experience

This process involves respecting the model of the world expressed by the other and demonstrating that one values and 'sees' their position without being at all judgemental. One does not have to agree with a person's map of the world, although it is important, if one wishes to build rapport, that one respects it. Dilts and Delozier (2000, p. 910) define pacing as *"the process of using and feeding back key verbal and non-verbal cues from the other person in order to match his or her model of the world"*. You cannot lead another unless you are prepared to pace their experience and map of the world. Pacing involves matching your experience of the world with that of the other. To pace effectively you would match the appearance, physiology and lead sensory system adopted by the other.

To achieve rapport, you must establish what it is that is important to you and to the other, and establish a common interest. You must also be sensitive to the world view of the other and respect differences in relation to your own. It is a good idea not to criticize their world view or reveal your own in terms of its differences. As you match and align your criterion with the other and respect their world view you are effectively pacing the other's experience of their world, their own map of reality. Once you are firmly established in your pacing strategy and rapport is also established, at least on the surface, you may then start to lead the other person slightly away from their fixed world view to accommodate your alternative perspective – if there is one – or to support the achievement of your criterion.

The art of pacing is regarded as a critically important aspect of NLP applications. It is also arguably a highly underestimated leadership process and, as such, is fundamental to the rapport-building process. Dilts and Delozier (2000, p. 909) continue:

> *Pacing is the process of feeding back to another person, through your own behaviour, the behaviours, and strategies that you have observed in that individual. Pacing involves recognizing and acknowledging another person's behaviour and model of the world.*

Basically, what you are trying to do when pacing is to complement the sense-making processes and emotional and cognitive states and strategies employed by your audience so that they feel at ease with you and confident, at an unconscious level, in your company. This degree of acceptance enables rapport-building processes. You are trying to respect and acknowledge the experience of the other person by describing their representational content through matching and listening.

Elicitation

Elicitation involves bringing forth the emotional content and mindset attached to an experience that a person has constructed. A good example of

142 *A model of rapport building*

the elicitation process would involve a group of people meeting to discuss a change project. One person is the change manager and the others are members of the general management team to whom the change leaders need to sell the idea of the change project. Each person may bring with them a unique thinking style which is imbedded in an emotional mindset. One could usefully call these thinking styles dynamic identity positions towards the idea of the change project. I say dynamic because the idea of elicitation is that one can elicit a different emotional mindset in a person and, thus, change the nature of their identity position towards the change project. For example, there may be a realist, a sceptic, a dreamer, or an optimist in the group. By calibrating thinking styles, one can pace each person's model and match their identity in subtle ways using suggestive language patterns. For example, when dealing with the critic one could say "*you know John it is well known that 70% of change programmes such as this often do fail*"; then one can turn to the optimist and say "*however, we are not only interested in why these fail we are also interested why the other 30% have such amazing success*".

Such language patterns do help build rapport even when faced with a challenging audience. Also, John must reflect on the way the change manager framed the prospects of success associated with a change programme. The change manager did not contradict John's model of the world, rather she paced it and offered a reframe which suggested to John that both ideas were true; change programmes often do not work, and, in some cases, they do work. Such a reframe means that John, if he thinks about the content, will shift his emotional state and his mindset. When we mix internal representations, we cannot help but create a new mindset.

Leading

Once you are in a state of rapport, you can make efforts to lead the other from their current state to another state of mind. This process involves effective elicitation. For example, if you wish a group to shift their state from being defensive to being curious, this is an attempt at leading in NLP terms. If you simply try to do this through the medium of monologue, unless you are a gifted orator, you may find leading challenging. If you apply the techniques of calibrating, matching, eliciting, and pacing your audience, and engage them in conversation you will have an improved chance at leading their shaping of their particular world view.

Leading is a very delicate process. It involves presenting your own 'perceptual position' to the others in a way that enables them to build a bridge between their own personal map of reality and the new map that you are introducing. If you do this in a way that is acceptable to the others, then you will be leading the client and will have successfully bridged between alternate perceptual positions. This is when you are in a state of generative dialogue and are effectively thinking together. Leading basically involves subtly changing from matching to offering different thought processes and behaviours and inviting the other to follow you. A test of whether you are leading or not is if you deliberately shift your posture or voice tone or speed and the other follows you, unconsciously matching, then you can be confident that not only are they in rapport with you, they are also following your mental strategies.

If the others follow your line of thinking and engage in dialogue with you, then you have successfully bridged and built rapport. This is a critical change leadership skill. It does not guarantee that others will simply fall in line and agree with the case for change and behave in a supportive manner, however, it does mean that they are open to dialogue and change. What you can be sure of as a change leader is that if you don't build rapport, you don't build perceptual bridges, you will not establish dialogue, and, in the absence of generative dialogue, you will not establish collaborative working and leverage the collective intelligence of the group.

Internal rapport

A central component of managing rapport is managing one's own internal rapport with one's self. This idea may at first seem odd; however, I think that it is key to understanding the secret behind relationship management. If one cannot get on with oneself. how one can realistically expect to build sustainable rapport with others? The aim of self-rapport management is to achieve a state of congruence between the unconscious mind and the conscious mind. For example, your conscious mind may rationalize that investing in a new house is a sensible thing to do, whilst your unconscious mind feels uncomfortable with this decision. This happens because the conscious mind can only accommodate 7 plus 2 or minus 2 pieces of information at any one time. In contrast, the unconscious mind holds all the life experience and associated knowledge we have and can make sense of this vast reservoir of knowledge at incredible speed. If our rational conscious sense-making is not congruent with our deeper unconscious sense-making we will feel uneasy, and this feeling of being uneasy manifests in our emotional state.

Another issue regarding the unconscious mind is that if something is troubling us, we are often unaware of the incremental influence this concern has on our emotional state. Thus, we enter a negative state unconsciously and this state manifests throughout our physiology; we literally signpost to the other our concerns through our facial expressions, our voice tone, our tonal marking, our general body language, our breathing and even our complexion. People unconsciously read, or calibrate these signals and, because of emotional contagions, they can often turn away from us and disable any rapport-building opportunity. In effect they will find us disagreeable. They will sense our internal lack of rapport and will perceive our efforts at relationship building as being incongruent with our emotional state. Thus, managing our internal emotional state is a critical aspect of rapport building.

144 *A model of rapport building*

Closing thoughts

The American theorist Nancy Dixon (1996) has studied the ways in which people generate dialogue together so that they may think together. She notes that how people relate together is fundamental to whether they will be able to think together. I invite you to consider rapport-building processes as the pre-requisite methodology you should enact in advance of dialogue. In fact, I do not think dialogical exchange is possible if people do not first enter a state of rapport. Rapport is a paradox. At one level the methods appear remarkably simple, yet it takes practice and skill to combine the methods together to build sustainable and meaningful rapport with others. Critically, rapport starts with oneself; its starts with the premise that we must learn how to be con-gruent internally in relation to our values, beliefs, and actions. From this congruence comes the state of mind that we need to project onto others our sincerity for building rapport. One can help the rapport-building process by accessing COACH state and, in doing so, one can leverage one's inner resources in a maximizing way.

For change managers, rapport-building skills are essential. The ability to build rapport with your peers, your customers, your team members, and your line managers is a source of substantial competitive advantage that can provide you with the edge over others who are competing with you for scarce resources and rewards. Rapport is fundamental to change management situations as it is the essence of leadership. Rapport involves two or more people being comfortable with one another and identifying positively with each other's agendas. People in rapport have considerable influence over one another and enjoy an alignment of perspectives and, so, are comfortable in their relationships

References

Carnegie, D. (1936) *How to Win Friends and Influence People*, Vermillion.
Dilts, B. R. and Delozier, J. (2000) *Encyclopedia of Systematic Neuro-Linguistic Programming and NLP New Coding*, NLP University Press.
Dixon, N. (1996) *Perspectives on Dialogue*, Center for Creative Leadership.
Isaacs, W. (1999) *Dialogue: The Art of Thinking Together*, Doubleday.
O'Connor, J. and Seymour, J. (1990) *Introducing NLP: Neuro Linguistic Programming*, Mandala.

15 Communication models

Introduction

A principle of NLP is the idea that *'the meaning given off is the meaning received'*, which means that we may think we know what we mean when we communicate; however, we do not know what our audience think we meant and how they construct their maps based on our utterances. Thus, we need a model of communication that operates with these facts. NLP provides such a comprehensive model. When one is leading a change project, one is always involved in sense-making work. Alvesson and Sveningsson (2015) employ the useful metaphor of everyday reframing to explain the function of change leaders at work. In their model, change takes place because of a negotiated discourse between people, through which reality is framed and reframed in a constant cycle of interpretation and re-interpretation.

When thinking about change leadership, Smircich and Morgan (1982, p. 258) argue that *'Leadership is realized in the process whereby one or more individuals succeeds in attempting to frame and define the reality of others.'* They interpret change leadership as a process fundamentally concerned with the framing of reality when they argue that leaders emerge as authentic: *'Because of their role in framing experience in a way that provides a viable basis for action, e.g., by mobilizing meaning, articulating, and defining what has previously remained implicit or unsaid, by inventing images and meanings that provide a focus for new attention, and consolidating or confronting, or changing prevailing wisdom.'* The main technology for this process is, of course, language and the main channels for selecting empirical data our sensory system. This chapter builds a model of NLP communication strategies that can enable effective stakeholder engagement during periods of change by understanding social construction processes imbedded in language and exploiting this understanding.

The map is not the territory

An important aspect of every day reframing is that we all live inside a subjective bubble. For example, you could think about your existence as a movie

146   *Communication models*

that you have produced, and continue to edit and produce in the theatre of your own mind. Imagine that you are the producer, director, and editor of your own life experience. Life in terms of an objective independent reality is not accessible to you, or to others. Your experience of life is a socially constructed movie made up of edited experiences that you delete, generalize, and distort to make sense of your experience and to act onto the world around you. Your productions are heavily biased in line with your values and beliefs and preferences. You carefully filter experiences for future processing. This is an un-nerving proposition, is it not? Yet it is a reasonable metaphoric description of what happens when we experience life. We are simply mapmakers. It also means that we assume that everyone else sees the world as we see it and that when we describe aspects of our experience to others that they will understand our meaning as they, we assume, live and experience the same world. Unfortunately, this is not the case; it is a dangerously flawed assumption and plagues change projects and undermines well intentioned communication with stakeholders. NLP practitioners are very open and comfortable with this proposition. For example, an important NLP presupposition states that:

> *The meaning of your communication is not simply what you intend, but also the response you get.*

This idea can represent a substantial change in basic assumptions in relation to the unconscious paradigm many change leaders have internalized regarding communication. The accepted premise is the illusion that when we speak we transmit our intended meaning and we assume that others will naturally comprehend our intended meaning. However, there are two elements to our communication:

1   Our intended meaning (the transmitter)
2   The received meaning (the receiver)

Every day reframing is a useful model because it implies that aligning meaning systems via communication strategies is a habitual and sensitive process; change leaders need to work hard at it, in a thoughtful way. Everything we say and do and everything we do not say or do can provide meaning to our audience. Some of the meaning our audience construct is aligned with our intentions and, unfortunately, some of it may be misaligned. The literature on communication is vast and it is outside the scope of this book to review it thoroughly. What we can do, though, is identify a model of communication that highlights the main filters that people use to make sense of things. Our filters are the devices we use to decide what aspects of our experience we pay attention to and what meanings we attach to these experiences. We do not make sense of our experience passively. On the contrary, we actively filter, arrange, and compose sense data into what we call in NLP circles our modality structures. In Organizational Science we call these our schemas, or our frames of reference, social constructions, or interpretive frames (Tsoukas & Chia, 2002).

Our filters

It is useful if the change leader has a model of the various filters that their audience will use to give meaning to the messages sent by the change leader. The seven main filters that influence our change leadership communications are:

1 Our values
2 Our beliefs
3 Our meta-programmes
4 Our identity
5 Our primary sense-making system
6 Our attitudes
7 Active dissociation from an experience

These filtering tools operate at an unconscious level and generate a powerfully effective unconscious bias that either protects and maintains reality frames and thus ensures we get the same social results or, alternatively, they can enable the production of generative change strategies.

As we are bombarded with an overwhelming volume of sense data that we cannot process, we have developed coping mechanisms which involve distilling sense data through a highly efficient filtering system which involves active deletion of data, distortion of data, and the generalization of data. Sociologists coined the terms selective representation and unconscious bias to explain two very powerful filters that rely on the nature of an individual and a group's belief and value system.

Selective representation and unconscious bias

When we hold well-formed beliefs that generate our values we tend towards the processes of data which support our belief system and we ignore data that does not support our belief and value system. This process of moving away from, or moving towards something is called a meta-programme. The nature of this meta-programme also reveals our unconscious bias. Here is an example.

A Director was invited to attend a series of staff focus groups during a change project. The focus groups had an average of ten managers in each of them and there were 40 organized over a period. For each focus group, there was a facilitator who recorded the question and answer (Q&A) sessions. The facilitator grouped each aspect of the Q&A under discreet headings such as 'what worked well; what needed improvement?' The director did not fully support the programme. He did not identify with its methods or with its aims. However, she had to be seen to be being supportive. During the focus groups, the participants, generally, were very positive about the change programme and felt comfortable expressing their views regarding

148 *Communication models*

> what could be improved. A full report was then constructed as an update for the executive management team. They never received this. The director chose not to share it. Instead what she did was emphasise in private conversations the critical aspects of the change project from the participants' view point.

I do not believe that the director consciously behaved this way. This was not a subversive strategy she deliberately chose. She was simply operating in line with her meta-programme to move away from the change programme. She was selecting data that supported her belief system that the project was too complicated and not necessary. And she demonstrated an active bias towards discrediting the project. She could not share the update reports because they did not confirm her unconscious bias. In doing all of this she was simply filtering out much of the data, distorting it, generalizing from it, and deleting much of it. This short example shows just how fragile meaning making is. Another significant filter is the representational system that a person relies on as their lead sensory system.

Working with representational systems

NLP has also studied a complementary area of communication, an understanding of which increases the effectiveness of the change leaders' communicating capabilities. This area of study and NLP practice concerns representational systems which are defined by Dilts and Delozier (2000, 1097) as 'the neurological mechanisms behind the five senses'. As communication is often cited in the literature as one of the top fault lines undermining change leadership processes then an awareness of the nature of representational systems is of benefit to change leaders.

We all know that we make sense of the world that we experience through our five senses, known in NLP circles by the acronym 'VAKOG' (visual, auditory, kinaesthetic, olfactory and gustatory). The lead sensory system is based upon which of the five sense systems a person relies to make sense of and convey their sense-making impressions of the world around them. They typically choose from:

- Visual sense making: interpretations through visual constructs
- Auditory sense making: interpretations through sounds
- Kinaesthetic sense making: interpretations through feelings
- Olfactory sense making: interpretations through tastes
- Gustatory sense making: interpretations through smells.

As infants we use all of our sensory systems and through time as we mature we start to depend on one or two favourites. In most of cases we settle on our lead sensory system.

Lead sensory system

The lead sensory system will be the one most relied upon. For example, if a person has a general tendency to perceive the world visually then they relate more effectively to another person who is also a dominantly visual sense-maker and communicator. This rapport occurs because not only do we rely on one dominant sensory system to make sense of the world, we also communicate this sense-making through language that is sensory-based in relation to the lead sensory system. The words we employ when using sensory based language are known as predicates.

Predicates

Predicates are sensory-based words. You can identify which is the preferred sensory system by listening to the predicates people employ as they talk. Predicates are sensory based words and phrases such as:

- I 'see' what you mean (visual predicate)
- I get the 'picture' (visual predicate)
- I 'hear' you 'loud' and 'clear' (two auditory and one visual predicate)
- I don't 'like' the 'sound' of your idea (one kinaesthetic and one auditory predicate)
- Let's 'take' this subject 'apart' (two kinaesthetic predicates)
- I 'get' your 'point' (two kinaesthetic predicates)
- I don't 'like' the 'feel' of this idea (two kinaesthetic predicates)
- I've got a good 'feeling' about this proposal (one kinaesthetic predicate)

The representational system we prefer operates as a meta-programme and drives the selective representation of reality we apply to the social world as well as influencing our unconscious bias. We are receptive to predicates that belong to our lead sensory system and less sensitive to those that do not. Put simply: we pick up seeing words if we are visually orientated; hearing words if we are audio orientated, and feeling words if we are kinaesthetically orientated. It is thus incumbent upon the change leader to reflect on their own preferred sensory system and practice using the ones they least prefer with the aim of moving easily between all three when communicating with a person or an audience.

If the change leader is engaging in a one-to-one session then they simply calibrate the preferred representational system of the other person and, if required, shift their own to complement their colleague. If the change leader is communicating with a group then they must move between all three representational systems, perhaps saying the same thing three times using different representational systems.

7 + or - 2 messages

Another significant filter is the ability of our conscious mind to process the information in the first place. At any given time, psychologists believe, we

150 *Communication models*

cannot manage any more than nine pieces of data and the general rule is that we can comprehend at a conscious level between five and nine separate messages. Thus, we have the communication principle of '7 + or - 2'. This means that if, as change leaders, we deliver presentations making the case for change that are enabled through PowerPoint, with dense data expressed in tables, diagrams, video, and text, then the intended audience will simply not absorb many of the intended messages.

If we concentrate on four or five core (meta) messages and we frame each of these using different representational mediums and associated predicates we will have a much-increased probability of getting our message across to our audience. This involves saying the same point in different ways throughout the presentation and ruthlessly cutting down on PowerPoint and dense script and using simple evocative images that are culturally relevant to the topic at hand. For example, let us take the main theme which could be 'we have a problem that is a collective problem that we need to fix'. For the visual sense makers, the change leader would say:

> *"Let me show you what our problem looks like and paint a picture of our shared future."*

He may use images that symbolize the problem, maybe a simple graph that plots a dramatic fall in sales.

Then, later, in the short presentation targeting the kinaesthetic sense makers he may say:

> *"Obviously as we get to grips together with our shared problem and take it apart it's up to us to decide how best to construct a solution that works for everyone."*

Then, again, for the audio sense makers using audio-based predicates:

> *"Thank you all for listening to me today. I know things don't sound good. I also know that the idea of a shared successful future chimes with you, so I am asking you to work with the wider team to build a shared solution that resonates with you as a reasonable approach."*

So, he has made the same point using three different representational systems. He could mix it up as follows:

> *"Let me show you what our problem looks like and paint a picture of our shared future if we don't look to solve it together. I know things don't sound good. I also know that the idea of a shared successful future chimes with you, so I am asking you to work with the wider team to build a shared solution that resonates with you as a reasonable approach. Obviously as we get to grips together with our shared problem and take it apart it's up to us to decide how best to construct a solution that works for everyone."*

The implications for communicating change leadership messages is that we need to think carefully about how to design our messages using multiple representational systems. If we are communicating to groups a mixed model approach is required. If dealing with an individual, we simply listen to their predicates and adjust our language to tune in to their lead representational system.

The meta-model

The meta-model is a language-based analytical tool that was developed by Bandler and Grinder (1975). Largely due to the incredible amount of sense data we experience, our mind naturally deletes information, generalizes from experiences, and distorts experiences. These three processes are incredibly useful as sense-making tools to enable action from decision making. However, when one is trying to lead change projects, deletion, generalization, and distortion methods can be a significant barrier to diagnosing change, designing change interventions, and leading the successful implementation of a change project. This is because, as change leaders, we need a deeper understanding of the nature of change dynamics so that we may obtain a richer perceptual map of the change territory and problems. We need this to develop greater behavioural flexibility. Another issue with deletions, distortions and generalizations is the way that they can frame reality in such a way that it paints an unfavourable picture of the change project or critical aspects of it.

Working with the meta-model

The meta-model is an NLP tool used to gain a fuller understanding of what people do and say; when used carefully it can trigger reflective thinking on the part of another which naturally takes them into their deeper unconscious mind to explore the richer meaning system called their deep structure that their surface structure meaning construction system filters through distortions, deletions, and generalizations. This process of linguistic exploration using the meta-model can 'loosen the lid' on an individual's reality constructions.

The meta-model provides us with categories of distortions, deletions, and generalizations so that when we hear these being used we can recognize them for what they are. The meta-model also provides corresponding linguistic strategies we can use to guide the reflective process in the form of well-formed questions. O'Connor and Seymour (2002, p. 92) describe the meta-model as consisting of *"a series of questions that seek to reverse and unravel the deletions and distortions and generalizations of language."* The meta-model is made up of at least 12 language identification categories each of which has relevant questions that can be applied by the change leader to access the deep structure meanings that underpin surface structure expressions. Distortions are classified in Table 15.1.

Table 15.1 Meta-model violations: distortions

Meta-model category	Description	Strategies for exploring distortions
Complex equivalent	Two statements that are considered to mean the same thing, e.g., "He is not looking at me, so he is not listening to what I say."	"How does this mean that?"
Presupposition	Ideas or statements that have to be taken for granted.	"What leads you to believe that...?"
Cause and effect	The assumption that one variable will cause the manifestation of another variable.	How exactly does this cause that? What would have to happen for this not to be caused by that?
Mind reading	The assumption that one knows what another person is thinking without direct evidence.	"How exactly do you know...?"

Meta-model violations: deletions

Meta-model category	Description	Strategies for exploring distortions
Unspecified noun	Nouns that do not specify to whom or to what they refer.	"Who or what specifically?"
Unspecified verb	Verbs that have the adverb deleted, they do not say how the action was carried out. The process is not specified.	"How specifically?"
Comparison	This strategy is an important change leadership asset.	"Compared with what?"
Judgement	When something is being judged but the relative standard is omitted or the people doing the judging deleted.	"Who is making this judgement?" "On what grounds are they making this judgement?"
Nominalization	Linguistic term for the process of turning a verb into an abstract noun.	Questions should be asked that turn the noun back into a verb.

Meta-model violations: generalizations

Meta-model category	Description	Strategies for exploring distortions
Modal operator of possibility	A linguistic term for words that denote what is considered possible (can, cannot, etc.).	"What would happen if you did?"
		"What would happen if you did not?" "What prevents you from...?"
Modal operator of necessity	A linguistic term for rules (should, ought, etc.).	"What would happen if you did?" "What would happen if you did not?"
Universal quantifier	Linguistic term for words such as 'every', and 'all' that admit no exceptions; one of the meta-model categories.	"Has there ever been a time when...?"

A worked example

For example, if a change participant were asked to comment on how they thought the programme was working they could make the following statement:

> "I think they could have made more effort to sell the change project to us. I know they don't think they needed to, but they did. Clearly this means that they don't feel a need to really engage with us. All that happens is people get more detached and less committed. Just look at the way the programme was rolled out... awful... just terrible. That's a pity though as it just goes to prove what we all know that these kinds of things don't really work... and I mean they never work. For example, if you look at the last time we tried this... I mean ... are they serious? Also, I don't think people are really committed to the project as we all have too much to do as it is. I suppose if they were listened to and involved more, then they would get motivated though this is not possible in this culture."

The above is an example of a meta-model exercise that can be used in an NLP for change leaders course. It is riddled with distortions, generalizations, and deletions. We can invite delegates to identify the meta-model violations imbedded in the text. Then they select appropriate meta-model questions. The meta-model, because of its usefulness for clarifying, challenging, and stimulating new ways of thinking, quickly became a central model used within standard NLP training courses. As an exercise, I invite you to analyse the statement and identify the list of meta-model violations it contains.

The meta-model primarily focuses on the idea that, when attempting to make sense of the world, it is a natural, human mechanism to generalize, distort and delete aspects of our experience; to cognitively filter reality in such a fashion that causes us to be selective in what we pay attention to. We can take a few specific experiences and transform them into broad judgements; twist the facts in a way that significantly alters and changes our representation of an event; and neglect elements of the full story of reality, creating gaps within the conscious recollection of our experience.

By actively listening for 'meta-model violations' – a term coined by Bandler and Grinder (1975) to describe linguistic statements containing either generalizations, distortions, or deletions – and then asking questions to clarify and encourage re-evaluation, the change leader can skilfully lead the participant through a process of self-realization and exploration into new and more useful ways of thinking, feeling and behaving. By artfully becoming aware of meta-model distinctions in the utterances people make, and then seeking clarification using the model's questions, it becomes possible to arrive at an enriched version of their reality; one that is largely free from generalizations, distortions, and deletions. The dominant principle behind the meta-model is that language use to represent reality is only a map of reality, it is not the territory.

Concluding thoughts

Our model of representational systems is based upon the premise that communication between people is akin to tuning in to a radio station. We have all heard the saying '*he is on a different wave length from me*' or '*they're just not on the same frequency*', such sayings are drawing our attention to incongruence between the way people are making sense of their world and communicating this sense-making to others. There can be many different reasons for this; however, one dominant reason is based on the sensory system we use to make sense of and communicate our sense-making to others. Another fundamental reason for lack of congruence is the influence that meta-model violations have on meaning construction. If we depend mainly on a visual sense-making scheme we will most likely communicate our sense-making via visual sensory based words. This could be regarded as the visual frequency. If I were to try to communicate with someone who uses the visual frequency through a kinaesthetic medium, i.e., I made sense of the world through feelings and used kinaesthetic sensory-based words, we would be on different sense-making frequencies and would not be able to tune in to each other, which thus hinders rapport-building opportunities. Therefore, change leaders need to be sensitive to representational channels and adjust their own frequency setting to tune in to the other person. Change leaders also need to be able to work sensitively and competently with meta-model violations.

If one considers the idea that many change leaders are unaware of sensory systems, predicates, frequency channels, filters, meta-model violations, or meta-model questions, then it should come as little surprise that communication is commonly cited as such a significant change management fault line. If change leaders are authentic and desire successful change then they could take time to learn the meta-model and study representational channels and develop highly sensitive listening skills to identify predicates and lead representational systems. Our choice of lead representational system and our decision to rely less on others act as filters to ensure that only selective aspects of experience are paid attention to. Thus, our sensory acuity is impaired by our decision to limit our competence in using all our sensory systems and to rely predominantly on one.

References

Alvesson, M. and Sveningsson, S. (2015) *Changing Organizational Culture*, Routledge.
Bandler, R. and Grinder, J. (1975) *The Structure of Magic*, Science and Behaviour Books Inc.
O'Connor, J. and Seymour, J. (2002) *Introducing Neuro-Linguistic Programming: Psychological Skills for Understanding and Influencing People*, Harper Element.
Smircich, L. and Morgan, G. (1982) Leadership: The Management of Meaning. *Journal of Applied Behavioural Science*, 18: 257–273.
Tsoukas, H. and Chia, R. (2002) On Organizational Becoming: Rethinking Organizational Change. *Organization Science*, 13: 567–585.

16 NLP and OD

Two not-so-distant relatives. It's time for collaboration

Introduction

> The difference between what we do and what we are capable of doing would suffice to solve most of the world's problems.
>
> Mahatma Gandhi

This chapter compares the genesis of both the NLP and organizational development movement (OD). I shall present a picture of the seminal moments that acted as developmental catalysts for the two areas of change work and demonstrate their remarkable similarities. I close by arguing that there is a strategic need for NLP to find a new sponsor to inject vitality and purpose into the field inclusive of a significant push towards high quality research into its effects as well as aiming towards continued development of its conceptual and practical architectures. The chapter closes with a principle that is common to both NLP and to OD, which is to be successful as a change s leader, one must model the change one wishes to see in the world.

NLP can be considered as a specialized area of personal and group development which has not followed the trajectory of the OD school of thought. If we compare the development of NLP and the OD movement we can clearly see dramatic similarities in their genesis. The discussion below highlights the historical milestones regarding the development of both the OD and NLP movements. Whilst some of the development highlights bear remarkable similarity, there remains a fundamental strategic difference that has had profound influence on the credibility and potential longevity of both schools of practice.

Genesis of the OD movement

This chapter draws from the work of French and Bell (1999) into organizational development. The chapter will mention OD developers though it will not explain their work as all I am doing is recognizing their involvement in the early OD training groups as a comparator with the development of NLP. All the OD developers mentioned, and their collective writings are cited by

156 *NLP and OD*

French and Bell. The OD movement was originally founded by accident by charismatic leaders such as Kurt Lewin, Ronald Lippitt, Kenneth Benne and Leland Bradford. They literally stumbled across OD as they were engaged in an action research project into race relations issues in Connecticut. They attracted followers to their new field such as Douglas McGregor, Herbert Shepard, Robert Blake and Jane Mouton, Chris Argyris, Warren Bennis and Richard Beckard, and others. Many of the early OD developers emerged as global leaders of the OD movement. These co-developers of OD were also students at leading US universities studying social science subjects. Together, these pioneers and their followers designed training and intervention programmes targeting group change work in both community and organizational settings. The early co-developers (especially Douglas McGregor) were, to varying degrees, influenced by the psychotherapist Carl Rogers and his ideas of client centred therapy. Further, the transdisciplinary influence of leading thinkers from political science, psychology, sociology, and anthropology also helped shape the development of the OD field. The pioneers initially referred to themselves as 'trainers' and they established a network of 'National Training Laboratories' (NTLs) throughout the USA. Douglas McGregor and Richard Beckard following their cultural change intervention into General Mills decided to call their new field OD as an abbreviation for organizational development as they were thinking about a 'systems wide' change, not personal and individual person-centred change work.

Through collaborations in Europe, particularly with Robert Trist at the Tavistock Institute in the UK, the network of NTLs spread across the world. The main emphasis was on action research. The base for the NTLs was to be business schools in universities. The aim was to develop models of both theory and practice which could be used by managers, supported by OD consultants trained and educated in the behavioural sciences to create cultural change within organizations leading to a more 'humane' form of organizational practices. The developers of the OD movement desired the design of organizational cultures that maximized both economic effectiveness and the potential for the self-actualization of the human spirit in practical terms.

Over the last 70 years the OD movement has firmly established itself in thousands of business schools throughout the world. It has developed industrial connections that are now deeply institutionalized in occupational groups such as personnel managers and HRM managers. OD is central to the continuous development of these groups of managers through institutes such as the Chartered Institute of Personal and Development. There are numerous undergraduate, masters' and PhD programmes emphasizing OD as their unit of study. Through the medium of academic research at masters' and doctorate level the field continues to develop and grow, and new intellectual leaders are being produced organically through the research and publication process. Finally, there is a healthy union between the field of OD, the practice of management, change and leadership throughout global industry.

OD has been a great gift to the world. The second great gift that the pioneers of the OD movement gave the world was the process of imbedding the movement within the institutions of university business schools. This has ensured its longevity. It has ensured a transfer of power to develop the field from the early pioneers and developers to a succession of future leaders and practitioners throughout the world.

Genesis of the NLP movement

As we know from Chapter 2 NLP was initially founded also by accident in the mid-1970s at the University of California Santa Cruz by three charismatic and curious men: John Grinder, Richard Bandler, and Frank Pucelik. They also stumbled across NLP as they were engaged in an action research project into how to model excellent practices demonstrated by people who consistently generate success in their field. They initially modelled three outstanding therapists, Virginia Satir, Fritz Perls, and Milton Erickson. Both Bandler and Pucelik were students at the University whilst Grinder was a professor in linguistics and a full-time faculty member. They attracted followers to their new field, such as Robert Dilts, Judith Delozier and Stephen Gilligan, who were students at the University of Santa Cruz. From what I can gather from the limited historical literature on the history of NLP deposited by the originators, the name Neuro-Linguistic Programming (NLP) was coined by Grinder and Bandler as they were perplexed as what they were going to call their new field, although the official history of this naming process remains a blurred affair.

Grinder et al., in collaboration with their followers, became global co-developers of NLP. As I understand the history, Robert Dilts, as a seminal developer, had a significant influence on the design of the first NLP practitioner and master practitioner training and intervention programmes targeting individual change work in community and organizational settings. This is a fundamental difference between the OD and NLP movements; OD targets group change and cultural change, whilst NLP targets individual change and social influencing processes. However, this difference is what excites me personally about the two fields: that is the idea of a collaborative convergence.

The original founders and developers of NLP were all influenced by the various fields of psychotherapy and the transdisciplinary influence of leading thinkers from political science, linguistics, psychology, sociology, and anthropology helped shape the development of the NLP field. Here is the second major distinguishing factor between the development of NLP and OD; NLP opted for commercial training schools, disassociated from university faculties offering practitioner certificates as convenient models of learning, targeting mass market appeal. The OD strategy in contrast was one of research and practice through university models of transmission and diffusion.

Through their network of 'franchised' NLP institutes, NLP grew exponentially throughout the world as a commercial product targeting the personal

158 NLP and OD

development market. The main emphasis was and remains on practice. This is the third substantial differentiator between the two fields. Whilst OD aimed to generate both theory and practical applications into group change and development, NLP publicly distanced itself from the academic approach and the emphasis on generating theory and created a hegemony that privileged practical applications that 'worked'. This strategy has characterized the field for over 40 years and may yet prove to be its nemesis. It has potentially stunted the potential for developing NLP as a distinctive body of knowledge and practice and has created an easy target for its critics. Charges of pseudo-science; non-evidence-based claims; and cult mentality are and continue to be directed against NLP. For example, famously, Wikipedia published the following statement regarding NLP:

NLP has since been overwhelmingly discredited scientifically, but continues to be marketed by some hypnotherapists and by some companies that organize seminars and workshops on management training for businesses. There is no scientific evidence supporting the claims made by NLP advocates and it has been discredited as a pseudoscience by experts. Scientific reviews state that NLP is based on outdated metaphors of how the brain works that are inconsistent with current neurological theory and contain numerous factual errors. Reviews also found that all of the supportive research on NLP contained significant methodological flaws and that there were three times as many studies of a much higher quality that failed to reproduce the "extraordinary claims" made by Bandler, Grinder, and other NLP practitioners. Even so, NLP has been adopted by some hypnotherapists and by companies that run seminars marketed as leadership training to businesses and government agencies.

Compare the above with the way that Wikipedia describes OD:

Organizational development as a practice involves an ongoing, systematic process of implementing effective organizational change. OD is known both as a field of applied science focused on understanding and managing organizational change and as a field of scientific study and inquiry. It is interdisciplinary in nature and draws on sociology, psychology, particularly industrial and organizational psychology, and theories of motivation, learning, and personality. Although behavioural science has provided the basic foundation for the study and practice of OD, new and emerging fields of study have made their presence felt. Experts in systems thinking, in organizational learning, in the structure of intuition in decision-making, and in coaching (to name a few) whose perspective is not steeped in just the behavioural sciences, but in a much more multi-disciplinary and inter-disciplinary approach have emerged as OD catalysts or tools. Organization development, as a growing field, is responsive to many new approaches.

According to my perspective, the Wikipedia account of NLP is understandable albeit potentially influenced by the writer's unconscious bias, given its self-admitted dissociation from academic research and its distancing from university-led critical study. However, from a personal experience of practicing and teaching NLP, I have a firm belief that the foundations of its methodology are solid and that many of its claims are valid. Yet, this anecdotal evidence is a paradox when it comes to defending the credibility of NLP as its critics often say that this is not 'hard' evidence, yet, paradoxically, in business faculties throughout the university world a qualitative approach to academic study into organizational change using the world view, experiential statements and perspectives of the individual manager is accepted as evidence in many peer reviewed journals. In fact, there is a growing call for the crafting and submission of 'auto ethnographic' accounts into change management, and/or leadership practices by the editorial boards of peer reviewed journals and a move away from quantitative studies into organizational behavioural change and a move towards qualitative experiential based subjective change work, the premise of NLP interventions.

The base for the NLP teaching faculties was to be commercial NLP schools operating under the control of a commercial institute, not a university. The aim, as I read the situation, was to make money and sell commercial training products and to make a difference in the world. This does not mean that the early pioneers and developers were not primarily interested in emancipatory projects – they were very much interested – it is to say that the commercial model dominates over the research orientation that the OD movement has maintained over the last 70 years. Yes, OD practitioners and consultants also aim to make money out of their products and they often market their products by emphasizing economically efficient benefits to their clients before emancipatory; however, I do feel that within the university faculties and implicit in much of the OD literature is an emphasis on humanistic values and gains.

NLP can be an emancipatory project

There is no doubt, though, that NLP is also at its heart an enabler for the realization of an emancipatory project. Within its techniques there is the promise of the freeing up of limiting beliefs that are damaging the quality of one's life experience and social relationships. Within NLP there is also the explicit aim of developing rapport between people to break down barriers based on ignorance and prejudice. NLP, as with OD, is interested in creating change dialogues; powerful dialogues either internal to self or external and between groups. These dialogues are the only way humans will resolve many of their differences and create open channels for developing emancipatory projects. In the world we live in today, and that of tomorrow, the need for social technologies that enable generative dialogue has never been greater.

160   *NLP and OD*

NLP and its global reach

Over the last 40 years the NLP movement has firmly established itself in NLP schools throughout the world. It has developed models of practice that are now deeply institutionalized in activities such as sales, leadership, personal and group change, teaching, and therapy. Unfortunately, there are few undergraduate, masters' and PhD programmes emphasizing NLP as their unit of study. Nevertheless, it must be stressed that NLP has had an enormous influence on the shaping of coaching and the development of coaching as an industry targeting individual and group change. Through the medium of popular books, the field continues to develop. However, in contrast with the OD movement. which imbedded the movement within the institutions of university business schools. NLP has failed to establish an organic model of reproduction and self-renewal that has a life force of its own beyond the influence of its founders. Yes, there are many NLP inspired projects being led by charismatic developers throughout the world today, though I cannot see how these will last. If they are not imbedded into an institutional learning structure allocated with university faculties with the theory and practice of NLP decoded and woven into degree programmes at undergraduate, post-graduate and doctorate levels then I worry that, through time, NLP may wither on the vine that produced it. We need, I think, an open dialogue between two very compatible fields of practice which at their hearts share a common philosophy interest which is a union between OD and NLP and, for me, this can only happen if NLP is accepted into and is motivated to join business school faculties as a legitimate area of academic study into the theory and practice of social and cultural change at the level of the individual and of the group. This strategy, for me, would ensure its longevity. As with OD this will ensure a transfer of power to develop the field from the early pioneers and developers to a succession of future leaders and practitioners throughout the world.

Closing comments: model the changes you want to see in others

On a closing note I would like to emphasize the importance of role modelling. To really learn how to do NLP one needs to be totally immersed in the culture of NLP. Delozier, a co-developer of the field, refers to this process as 'getting NLP into your muscles'. This is a process of developing what Bourdieu (1991) called a 'cultural habitus', literally imbedding the NLP philosophy and methodologies into your emotional, cognitive, and behavioural expressions. Doing NLP should be an automatic cultural response to any given social situation. This kind of NLP autopilot needs to be nurtured if it is to develop. Through time, with constant practice at a level of conscious competency you will practice NLP at an unconscious level just as you drive a car from A to B over long distances and have little conscious recollection of the driving process, yet, generally, you arrive safely at your destination. This level of practice, what we call unconscious competence, is the hallmark of learning.

Yes, absolutely one can model the exercises and internalize the ideas contained throughout this book and achieve breakthrough results; however, if you are a manager with a powerful interest in OD and you wish to develop NLP-inspired courses for your management community then you do need to train as an NLP practitioner, trainer, and developer. You need to '*be the change you want to see in your world*'.

References

Bourdieu, P. (1991) *Language and Symbolic Capital*, Polity Press.
French, W. L. and Bell, C. H. (1999) *Organizational Development*, 6th edn, Prentice Hall.

Index

Locators in *italics* refer to figures and those in **bold** to tables. The acronym NLP is used to refer to neuro-linguistic programming.

7 + or – 2 messages 149–51

age, demographic change 23–4, 30
agency 67; *see also* free will
airplane mode 71
Alvesson, M.: cultural change 37–8; experience 115–16, 124–5; meaning-making 7; meaning reconstruction 54; psychological safety 88
anchoring 47–8, 97–8
Anderson, Dean and Linda: conscious leaders 4–5, 12, 24; ego 42–3, 44; mindset 94
anthropology 46
applied sociology 19–21
Argyris, Chris 51
Aristotle Research Project (Google) 25–6, 27–9, 86
attitudes: emotional states 55–6; free will 67–8; mindset 101–2; *see also* COACH state; CRASH state
audit: COACH state 132–3; meta-programmes 107, **108–12**
authority 117–19

Bandler, Richard: meta-model 6, **152**; modelling behaviour 45; neuro-linguistic programming movement 15–17, 157; psychological safety 126–7
behavioural competencies 9–11
behavioural flexibility 121
belief systems 48, 53, 65–6, 98–99
Bell, C. H. 155–6
Black Box of social interaction 87
Bodenhamer, D. 103

body language 70, 92, 95, 127, 137, 140, 143
brain, neuro-linguistic programming 13–15
business schools 21–2, 156–7
butterfly effect 40–50

calibrated loops 139–40
calibration, rapport 138–40
caretaking 88, 126–34
Carnegie, Dale 11, 137
Castaneda, Carlos 33
change, case for 75–84
change challenges 23–6
change leadership 12, 39; birth of reflective practitioners 10–11; business schools 21–2; communication models 145; confessional 7–8; conscious leaders 4–6; context of this volume 11–12; definition 3–4; ethnocentric map making 36–9; language 14–15; 'map is not the territory' 9–10, 31–3, 64–5; meta-reflection 6–7; mindset 97, 100–1, 103; modalities 35; origins 8–9; psychological safety building 86–7; rapport building 135; reframing 34–5, 122–3; reprogramming 35; social construction 36; sub-modalities 35–6; territory 9–10; world views 33–4
change mantras 48, 98–9
chunking down, meta-programmes **106**, 112–3
chunking up, meta-programmes **106**, 112–3
client centred therapy 126–7, 156

Index 163

COACH state: audit 132–3; building 130–3; energy management 129–30; Law of Requisite Variety 61–2; reframing 122, 123; stacking emotional states 131
coaching containers 129
cognitive flexibility 121
communication: models of 145–54; responses to 70
confessional change leadership 7–8
conscious leadership: confessional 7–8; definition 4–6; ego 43; meta-reflection 6–7, 43, 44; mindsets 24; responsibility for actions 67; success factors 27–8; *see also* change leadership
content reframing 34
context reframing 34
controversy, neuro-linguistic programming 17–18
CRASH state: Law of Requisite Variety 61–2; psychological safety 127; reframing 122; stacking emotional states 131
cross-over mirroring 140
culture: butterfly effect 41; ethnocentric map making 36–9; non-judgemental principle 59–60; paradigm of NLP 64; programming 15
curious type **106**

DeLozier, Judith: calibration 138–40; conscious leaders 27; matching 140; neuro-linguistic programming movement 16, 157; pacing experience 141; rapport 135–6
demographic change 23–4, 30
Derks (2005) 14
dialogue, and rapport 138, 144
diffusion model: change leaders 4; ethnocentric map making 37
Dilts, Robert: airplane mode 71; calibration 138–40; COACH state 130; Law of Requisite Variety 51–2; matching 140; meta-programmes 107; neuro-linguistic programming movement 16, 157; pacing experience 141; psychogeography 133; rapport 135–6; SOAR model 76–83
disengagement epidemic 86
Dixon, Nancy 133, 144
DNA 137
downtime, Law of Requisite Variety 60–1
Dweck, Carol 95
dynamic, meta-programmes **105**

Edmondson, Amy 27
education, business schools 21–2, 156–7
ego 42–4
elicitation 141–2
emotional contagion 127
emotional flexibility 121
emotional states: internal rapport 143; Law of Requisite Variety 55–6; management 55–6, 88; somatic anchors 97–9; stacking 130–1
energy management 129–30
Erickson, Milton H. 16, 56–7, 157
ethnocentric map making 36–9, 59–60
experience: framing of 115–25; rapport building 141
experiential frames 122; *see also* framing

failure, understanding 65–6, **105**
feedback 65–6, 90–2, **105**
filters, communication 147–53
'fish and stretch' 90–2
flexibility, perceptual positions 121
framing: experience 115–25; psychological safety 89–90
Frankl, E. V. 67–8
free will: attitudes 67–8; emotional states 55–6
French, W. L. 155–6
future self 57–8

Gallwey, Timothy 7
Generation X 23–4
generative dialogue 138
genetic predispositions 137
Gestalt Therapy 15
Gilligan, Stephen 157
global reach, neuro-linguistic programming 160
Google study of success factors 25–6, 27–9, 86
Grinder, John: meta-model 6, **152**; micro interactive strategies 19; modelling behaviour 45; neuro-linguistic programming movement 15–17, 157; psychological safety 126–7
group context, butterfly effect 41–2
guiding 126–34

Haddock, G. 101
Hall, M. 103
hierarchy of needs 42
Holon, perception as 42, 44

164 Index

identity: change leaders 3–4; conscious leaders 4–6; ethnocentric map making 36–9; future self 57–8; Law of Requisite Variety 55
individual context, butterfly effect 41–2
integrity 40–1, 100, 117, 121
intentions, understanding 69
internal rapport 143
in-time meta-programmes **106**

judgemental type **106**
jungle gym tool 82

language: elicitation 142; ethnocentric map making 37–8; feedback 92–3; meta-model 151–3; neuro-linguistic programming 14–15, 20; psychogeography 133; somatic anchors 97–9
Law of Requisite Variety 51–2, 62; COACH versus CRASH 61–2; emotional states 55–6; future self 57–8; modelling excellence 56–7; non-judgemental principle 59–60; rapport building 60; reconstruction 54; reframing 123–4; regression in meaning systems 58–9; resources to manage problems 59; social construction 52–4; social identities 55; uptime and downtime 60–1
lead sensory system 10, 54, 141, 149
leadership *see* change leadership; conscious leaders; modelling behaviour
leadership styles 37–9
leading, rapport building 142–3
linguistic, meaning of 14–15; *see also* neuro-linguistic programming
Logical Levels Model 79–82, *80*
Lorenz, Edward 40

Maio, R. G. 101
management: change challenges 25–6; conscious leadership matters 27–8; context 11–12; demographic change 23–4, 30; emotional states 55–6, 88; Google success factors 25–6, 27–9; new practices 23, 29–30; psychological safety 26–7, 29
mantras 48, 98–9
'map is not the territory': change leadership 9–10, 31–3, 64–5; communication models 145–7
Maslow, A. H. 42

matching 46–7, 140
MBA programmes 21–2
McGregor, Douglas 99–100, 156
meaning-making 7, 115–16
meanings: psychological safety 89–90; reconstruction 54; regression in meaning systems 58–9; shift in perceptual position 70; social construction 52–4; social identity 55
meetings, models of the world 33
memories, regression in meaning systems 58
meta-messages 128–9
meta-model 6, 151–3, **152**
meta-programmes 9–10, 53, 102; audit checklist 107, **108–12**; choice of 107–13; kinds of 104–7, **105–6**; mindset 102–3, 104, 114
meta-reflection: conscious leaders 6–7, 43, 44; mindset 94–5, 99
micro interactive strategies 19
Millennials 24
Mindfulness Movement 61
mindset: attitudes 101; beliefs 99; conscious leaders 24; defining 95–6; elicitation 141–2; meta-programmes 103, 104, 113–4; meta-reflection 94–5, 99; Modality Frame Directive 96–7; psychological safety 88; somatic anchors 97–9; values 100–1
mindset mix analysis 95–6, **96**
mirror neurons 46
mirroring 140
modalities: change leadership 35–6; Law of Requisite Variety 53; mindset 96–7; regression in meaning systems 58–9
Modality Frame Directive 96–7
modelling behaviour: butterfly effect 40–1; Law of Requisite Variety 56–7; meaning of 45–50; resources to manage problems 68–9
Morgan, G. 145

National Training Laboratories (NTLs) 156
needs hierarchy 42
neuro, meaning of 13–14; *see also* neuro-linguistic programming
neuro-linguistic programming: applied sociology 19–21; business schools' evolution 21–2; butterfly effect 41; case for change 75–84; context 8–9; controversy 17–18; definition 13–15; ego 43; as emancipatory project 159;

Index 165

future self 57–8; genesis of movement 157–9; global reach 160; history of 15–17; language 14–15, 20; Law of Requisite Variety 51–61; meta-reflection 6–7; non-judgemental principle 59–60; and organizational development movement 155–61; as paradigm 64–71; rapport building 16, 29, 60; resources to manage problems 59; social construction 31; success of 17–19; user-friendliness 18
neurological levels model 76, 78, 80, 82
non-judgemental principle 59–60

O'Connor, J. 13, 34, 60
OD (organizational development) movement 126–7, 155–61
ontological flexibility 121
ontology 31
organizational development (OD) movement 126–7, 155–61
Organizational Learning 51, 66
organizational performance 12

pacing experience 141
paradigms, world of work 23–4
people management 8–10; *see also* rapport building
perceptions *see* meanings
perceptual filters 31–3
perceptual positions: experience 121; leading 142–3; meta-programmes 107–13, *112*; rapport building 70; SOAR model 79, 82
performance indicators, rapport 136–7
Perls, Fritz 15, 16, 157
Personal Mastery 51
personal relationships: modelling behaviour 45–50; rapport as indicator 136–7; significant others 46; *see also* rapport building
philosophy, experience 115
positive intentions 69
positivism 115
practitioners of NLP 18
predicates 10, 54, 57, 149, 150–1
programming, meaning of 15; *see also* neuro-linguistic programming
'providing fish and stretch' 90–2
psychogeography 133
psychological safety: building 86–93; caretaking 126–8; management 26–7, 29

Pucelik, Frank 15, 157
pulse checks 28–9

rapport building: author understanding 9, 10; definition 135–6; demographic change 24; Law of Requisite Variety 60; model of 135–44; neuro-linguistic programming 16, 29; psychogeography 133; psychological safety 89, *89*; resistance 70–1
reflexivity: birth of reflective practitioners 10–11; meta-reflection 6–7
reframing 34–5, 122–3, 146
relationship management 8–10; *see also* rapport building
repetitive behaviour 101–2, *101*
representation, selective 147–8
Requisite Variety *see* Law of Requisite Variety
resistance, rapport building 70–1
resources to manage problems 59, 68–9
respect for others 69
responsibility for actions 66–7
ripple *see* butterfly effect
risk, meta-programmes **105**
Rogers, Carl 126, 156

safety *see* psychological safety
Satir, Virginia 15, 16, 157
S.C.O.R.E. model 83–4, **85**
selective representation 147–8
self: butterfly effect 40–1; ego 42–4; in future 57–8
Senge, Peter 51, 52
sensemaking 7, 115–16
sensory system 10, 14, 53, 145, 148–9; *see also* lead sensory system
7 + or – 2 messages 149–51
Seymour, J. 13, 34, 60
significant others 46
Smircich, L. 145
S.O.A.R. model 76–83, *78*
social construction: change leadership 31–4, 36; experience 115, 119; future self 57–8; Law of Requisite Variety 52–4; neuro-linguistic programming 18–19
social context, butterfly effect 41–2
social identity *see* identity
social skills, rapport as 137
sociology 19–21
somatic anchors 97–9
soul 42–4
stacking emotional states 130–1

166 *Index*

state management 55–6, 88
state of being 6
static, meta-programmes **105**
strategies: experience 116, 117–18;
Law of Requisite Variety 52; neuro-linguistic programming 18–19; SOAR model 81
styles: feedback 92–3; leadership 37–9
sub-modalities 35–6, 53
success: Google study 25–6, 27–9, 86;
neuro-linguistic programming 17–19
Sveningsson, S.: cultural change 37–8;
experience 115–16, 124–5;
meaning-making 7; meanings 54;
psychological safety 88
systems theory: butterfly effect 40; Law of Requisite Variety 51

Taylorism 11–12
theory X 100
theory Y 100
therapy: neuro-linguistic programming 15–16; organizational development (OD) movement 156; psychological safety 126–7

through-time meta-programmes **106**
timeline, SOAR model 78, 82–3
toxic meta-messages 128–9
trainers of NLP 18
transmission model: change leaders 4;
ethnocentric map making 36–7, 38;
experience 117–18
Trist, Robert 156

unconscious bias 147–8
unconscious mind 143
unconscious modelling 48–9
uptime, Law of Requisite Variety 60–1
user-friendliness 18

validators, meta-programmes **105**
value systems 53, 64, 100–1, 116, 147
visual anchors 98
voice tone 70, 92, 137, 143

ways of being 5–6
Wikipedia statements 158–9
will, emotional states 55–6
world views: change leadership 33–4;
respecting others 69